'If you're looking for healthy food that is absolutely delicious, this book is exactly what you need. Sam's recipes are some of the most creative, beautiful and delicious ones I have come across. You can feel the love and attention to detail that goes into every single one of her creations.'
KIM, @BESTOFVEGAN

•••

'Sam's food always gets me to stop what I'm doing and just stare at the recipe photos. Every time I think she's outdone herself once and for all, she comes up with something even more spectacular and drool-inducing. Creative, honest and relatable, both Sam and her work are beacons of inspiration for anyone interested in living a life filled with good vibes and good grub.'
EMILY, THIS RAWSOME VEGAN LIFE

•••

'Sam's work in the vegan community (and beyond) is groundbreaking. Her images, her recipes and her style is fresh, innovative and eye-catching. I'm in love.
DANA, THE MINIMALIST BAKER

•••

'Sam's passion for crafting plant-based recipes is evident each time I see her work. She's a true inspiration to the vegan community!'
AMANDA, @RAW_MANDA

Beautifully
REAL FOOD

GUILT-FREE, MEAT-FREE RECIPES TO INDULGE IN

SAM MURPHY

BLINK
bringing you closer

This book is dedicated to your inner child.

The one who eats for pleasure.
The one who eats for nourishment.
The one who eats for an emotional safety blanket
(yes, we've all been there).
The one who eats for enjoyment with family and friends.
The one who, simply, just eats.

Published by Blink Publishing
3.25, The Plaza,
535 Kings Road,
Chelsea Harbour,
London, SW10 0SZ

www.blinkpublishing.co.uk

facebook.com/blinkpublishing
twitter.com/blinkpublishing

HB – 978-1-911274-28-5
TPB – 978-1-911274-93-3
eBook – 978-1-911274-27-8

A CIP catalogue of this book is available from the British Library.

Designed and typeset by Smith & Gilmour Ltd
Printed and bound in Lithuania

13 5 7 9 10 8 6 4 2

Papers used by Blink Publishing are natural, recyclable products made
from wood grown in sustainable forests. The manufacturing processes
conform to the environmental regulations of the country of origin.

Every reasonable effort has been made to trace copyright holders of
material reproduced in this book, but if any have been inadvertently
overlooked the publishers would be glad to hear from them.

Blink Publishing is an imprint of the Bonnier Publishing Group
www.bonnierpublishing.co.uk

DISCLAIMER:
The recipes and information in this book have been created for
the ingredients and techniques indicated. The publisher/author is
not responsible for any specific health or allergy needs that require
supervision nor any adverse reactions you may have to the recipes
in this book – whether you have followed them as written or have
modified them to suit your dietary requirements. Any nutritional
advice and information provided in this book is based on the author's
own experiences, research and knowledge. The information
provided is not to be used in place of proper medical advice.

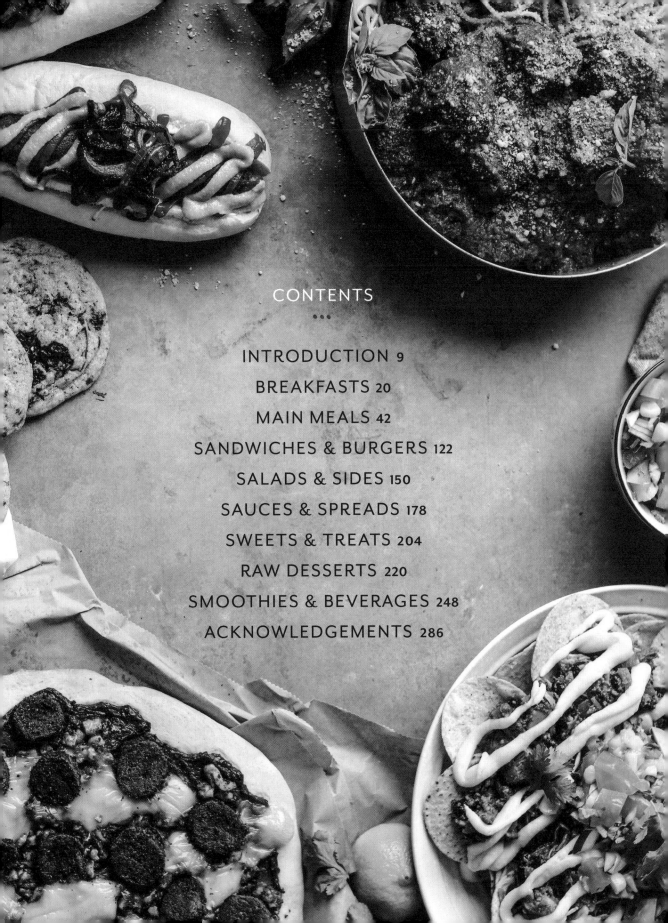

CONTENTS

•••

INTRODUCTION

...

I found veganism and the world of plant-based eating around
four years ago after spending years consumed in a 'tug-of-war'
relationship with food and my body. After years of struggling
to keep afloat, I had finally found something that grounded me
and pushed my boundaries – in only the most positive of ways.

With the removal of meat and dairy from my diet, I began the
quest in my kitchen to replicate my favourite meals in a way that
was not only for the most part healthy (hey, a girl still needs her
treats!), but also simple and enjoyable.

Along the way, I have shared my findings, my creations and my
honest and 'real' experiences across my social media platforms
(and now inside this book). I only wish that more people in the
world could realise how easy it is to make delicious, vegan food –
and that you can, I repeat, you CAN enjoy all of your favourite
classics, including meaty, cheesy and greasy flavours, and textures
all the way up to the sweet decadence of something like cheesecake
– minus the cruelty and numerous unhealthy side effects.

Each dish in this book reflects my journey thus far – a journey
of exploration, curiosity, love and finding a happy balance between
eating for health and eating for comfort, both physically and
emotionally, because food should offer nothing but enjoyment
on all levels.

I wish to provide you with the inspiration to create and the
tools to explore your own cooking quest with courage. I encourage
anyone and everyone to get in the kitchen, no matter how good
or bad you think you are – we all start somewhere, and we are all
a continuous work in progress, capable of changing for the better.
I think that's pretty magical.

MY STORY

•••

Food has meant many things to me over the years. It has been my greatest teacher, my greatest enemy, my ally, my best friend, my destroyer and my nurturer. My journey to veganism, to health and finding a sense of 'balance' with food and life as a whole has had its own set of challenges, yet it has also been single-handedly one of the most rewarding experiences of my life.

Let's track back 10 years. I grew up in in the South Island of New Zealand, which will forever hold a special place in my heart. I lived your 'picture perfect' Kiwi childhood – eating copious amounts of fish and chips, hokey pokey ice cream and mince and cheese pies. As a kid I was showered with the love and generosity of my parents and wider family, and I'm truly thankful for having had such a fantastic childhood. I can trace my love and passion for cooking to the many hours I spent in the kitchen with my mother, cooking for the family (I think I mostly just liked eating the batter and dough left in the bowl after baking cookies and cakes). For the most part, my adolescent years were spent enjoying carefree and fun-filled times. But, as any young girl does, I hit puberty. Things suddenly didn't seem so innocent and carefree. My body started changing. I felt different. I was experiencing new emotions, and I wasn't quite sure how to process it all.

It was at around this age that I felt a desperate urge to try and control all that was changing around me, mainly the curves I could feel multiplying on my hips. This desire for control flung me headfirst into a battle with a series of eating disorders and body dysmorphia, swinging from one end of the spectrum to the other by either binge eating or attempting diets of starvation. I was incredibly unhappy, lonely and fixated with nothing other than my looks and the food on my plate.

I knew I couldn't live the rest of my life this way, so I set out on a quest to try to find a solution to the power struggle I was facing between my food and myself. On this 'quest' I spent a few years dancing with various trends that (at the time) I thought would help me find the sense of balance and the happiness I was so eagerly seeking – fitness modelling, low-carbohydrate diets, fasting and supplements, to name a few. The list grew longer, yet I was digging myself deeper and deeper into a hole that was going to be increasingly harder to crawl out of.

I stumbled across veganism by accident in late 2013. While trekking through the internet, a few videos on YouTube caught my eye. I was instantly sold on the promise that I could eat as much as I wanted, stay slim and heal my metabolism. It all sounded too good to be true.

Initially, I got it all very, very wrong. I had no real clue what 'vegan' truly meant, because all I heard and decided to follow was the guideline that I could eat as many calories as I wanted. I was completely unaware of any ethical, environmental or general health benefits that accompany a vegan diet. This was, once again, solely driven by a desire to look a certain way. In my mind, this all equated to me being able to fit as much pasta into my body as I physically could in one sitting. Don't get me wrong, I'm all for eating large, wholesome quantities of food and enjoying meals without restrictions – however, what I was consuming was not providing me with any essential nutrients. I was ignoring all of my natural hunger signals, feeling extremely lethargic and confused.

In the midst of my frustration, I began searching deeper for another solution and fell into the world of raw veganism. Without delving into too much detail, I can attest that eating a diet of solely raw foods left me feeling physically amazing – energised, lean and glowing – but the trade-off was that it didn't pair well with my perfectionist personality or my past history. I became even more fixated on what I was consuming and the purity of my food, and I even became afraid of eating foods that were high in fat or cooked. The intensive list of food rules I had already curated multiplied, and soon enough I realised that this wasn't sustainable and I didn't want to live my life this way (nor was I any fun to be around).

During this time, I moved overseas to Melbourne. Starting afresh in a new country was exciting, and I made the choice that I didn't want my relationship with food and my body to hold me back and stop me from experiencing the joys that Melbourne had to offer. The change didn't happen overnight, but slowly I began introducing a wider variety of plant-based wholefoods into my diet. I faced my fear of certain foods that I had placed on the taboo list and attempted to relax around my strict and regimental eating routine.

The mission that I had embarked on a year earlier transitioned from the sole focus of trying to control my weight through extreme methods to seeking a balance between eating for health and eating for pleasure.

• • ·

My food, and the recipes in this book, are a very direct reflection of my journey, my creativity and my beliefs. It's the closest part of me I can share with you. I truly believe that food should and can simply be enjoyed, minus the cruelty. If you don't enjoy eating something, don't eat it!

After removing the 'Good versus Bad' mentality that had controlled my life for years, I noticed a huge shift in my appreciation and love for food. Food has now become a source of self-love instead of a tool for self-depreciation and control – love the food you eat and that food will love you back!

By removing labels and breaking down restrictions, while maintaining my desire to keep what's on my plate cruelty-free and sustainable, I actually made way for an influx of creativity, allowing me to really explore different ways of eating plant-based food and thus found what really works for me.

I'm by no means perfect – what I eat varies week to week, it's always changing and I have learnt that this is okay and to simply move and dance with my appetite instead of fighting and suppressing it. Some days I still face past problems, however, I have learnt to appreciate and welcome the challenges and the lessons they bring me.

We are all so wonderfully unique, and what's good for me may not be good for you – hence, with this book, I invite you to explore what works for you and to try new things in the kitchen, to be courageous and challenge your own belief system surrounding food. And, most importantly of all, to simply enjoy what is on your plate.

ADDITIONAL INFORMATION

•••

MY RECIPES

In this book you will find a wide variety of plant-based recipes ranging from everyday staples to delicious treats. I don't believe in labelling food as 'good or bad' – but I do 100% promote that you take the time to indulge as well as take the time to find what works for your own body and sensitivities by using your own discernment, judgement and intuition.

SENSITIVITIES/ALLERGIES

I understand that this day and age a lot of us face a variety of food allergies and sensitivities. Now, I would have loved to provide an alternative for every allergy – but that would require another book in itself. If there is something you cannot have in a recipe (i.e. gluten and soy, both of which are products I consume and cook with regularly and have no issues with) and if I have not stated an alternative, I invite you to research and find the best alternative for your climate, budget and body. However, please keep in mind that by substituting an ingredient in my recipes (mainly baked goods and raw desserts) it can result in the finished product producing a different taste and texture.

CONVERSIONS, MEASURING & BAKING

Everything in this cookbook has been measured using a Standard Australian Cup. The Australian cup (250ml) is a little different from the US cup (240ml) and the UK cup (225ml) so please keep this in mind when making any recipes. When measuring dry ingredients like flour, please ensure you spoon the flour into the measuring cup as opposed to scooping the measuring cup straight into the bag.

It is also important to note that I bake and cook with a conventional gas oven, so please be mindful of the variation in temperatures especially if you are cooking with a fan-assisted oven.

EQUIPMENT

There are really only two things that I swear by in the kitchen (aside from the staple pots and pans) and that is a good-quality sharp knife and a high-quality blender. These two investments truly have opened so many doors in my culinary adventures! I do understand that these aren't exactly budget-friendly, but I do encourage you to shop around for second-hand blenders or refurbished blenders! It's a great investment and will truly take your vegan food game to the next level! (For those who are interested, I use an Optimum Series blender.) A high-powered blender will ensure you get super smooth, silky and creamy sauces, cheesecakes and spreads – and their sturdiness will tackle harder to blend ingredients like nuts, coconut oil and whole vegetables with ease!

INGREDIENTS

•••

If you are new to plant-based cooking in general, there may be a few ingredients and methods in this book that you haven't heard of before. Here's a quick list of more 'uncommon' ingredients. Most of these will be available at your local health food store, vegan sections in most markets and grocery stores and online (Amazon, iHerb.com etc). If all else fails, a quick Google search of the ingredient you are after followed by your location can usually locate the best place for you to purchase from.

Nutritional Yeast Flakes

These are little golden flakes of vegan magic. Nutritional Yeast is a vegetarian supplement that is rich in B-vitamins. It has a strong 'cheesy' flavour. I use it regularly to add 'cheesiness' to cheese sauce and you'll find it used a lot throughout this book. It can be sprinkled over popcorn or salads, added to juice, cereal, smoothies, soups or sometimes I just like sprinkling it over my meal (or myself).

Liquid Smoke

This is a concentrated seasoning used predominately to flavour meat and fish. However in the 'vegan world' it is widely used to season mock meats, tofu or tempeh – anything really that calls for a smokey, BBQ aroma. Use it sparingly, as it is quite strong! If you can't find liquid smoke in your area, substitute with Spanish smoked paprika to add a similar taste to your meal.

Vegan Cheese

Vegan cheese substitutes are becoming more readily available worldwide. There are a lot of different varieties, from grated cheese to whole blocks of cheese. I have found that some vegan brands (I usually use 'Daiya' or 'BioCheese') do not 'melt' like regular cheese, and you can be left with the cheese shreds still looking intact.

To get around this I simply melt 2 cups of finely grated vegan cheese in a small non-stick saucepan with 3–4 tablespoons (or more) of plant-based milk over a medium heat. Whisk continuously over the heat until all the cheese has melted (around 2–3 minutes), the lumps are gone and it forms a silky, smooth and stretchy cheese sauce! Whisk in more plant-based milk if you'd like it thinner. Simply spoon or drizzle if over whatever it is that you need melted cheese on!

It's even better after these steps and then placed in the oven and grilled (depending on the recipe you're using it for).

Anyway, this is simply a personal preference of mine and you don't have to do this! I just like doing it this way as it gives me melted, stretchy cheese just the way I like it. Please be aware that brands of cheese will vary depending on what ingredients they are made from, so use your own discernment and add more or less liquid as needed when in the saucepan. This also means that the consistency of the cheese will vary when melted depending what brand you use.

Mock Meats

Although I have included a recipe for creating your own mock meat (seitan) at home, it can be less time consuming and easier to purchase pre-made mock meats. I enjoy mock meats on occasion; it's a fun and creative addition to meals and great for those transitioning to a vegan lifestyle. However, it should not override the importance of whole fruits and vegetables. The tastes and textures of mock meats simply 'imitate' that of meat; if you are new to mock meats, keep in mind that some textures you will prefer and some you won't – it's all about finding which you prefer!

Jackfruit

A few of my recipes require 'young green jackfruit' in water or brine, which can be purchased at most Asian grocers or online at Amazon. Please ensure it is the 'young green' kind, not the syrupy one! Jackfruit is simply an Asian fruit with a mild sweet taste, and the canned variety, once cooked and prepared properly, can resemble shredded chicken or pork. It is virtually tasteless and will absorb any flavour you cook it in.

Soaked Cashews

You will notice a few recipes in this book call for raw cashews that have been soaked for 3–6 hours (mainly for my raw cakes and sauces). This is simply to soften and activate the cashews which is going to make them blend smoothly, allow them to be more easily digested and make their nutritional content more readily available. To soak cashews for my recipes, I simply pop the required amount in a jar or container, fill it with filtered water, seal the jar and refrigerate for 3–6 hours. Ensure you drain and rinse the cashews from their liquid before using them in recipes. I am aware that raw nuts and seeds may

be expensive where you live, so try to bulk-buy ingredients when you can! When shopping for cashews, keep an eye out for bulk bags of 'broken cashew pieces' – these are just all of the broken, not-so-pretty cashews. They are generally sold at a discounted price, so ask your local grocer or health-food store if they stock them or can point you in the right direction.

NOTE: An activated nut is one that has been soaked (sprouted) and then dehydrated to release its enzyme inhibitors, making them easier to digest. It is preferable to use activated walnuts because it softens the walnut giving it a 'meat-like' texture. However, regular walnuts are okay to use as long as they are ground into smaller pieces.

Flaxseed Meal

Flaxseed meal (or linseed meal) is simply ground flaxseeds, which have been ground into a meal. You can do this yourself by blending flaxseeds in a high-powered blender until a fine powder forms. Flaxseed meal is mainly used as an egg replacement in vegan baking. Simply mix 1 tablespoon flaxseed meal with 3 tablespoons water and allow to sit for 10 minutes – this will work as a substitute for 1 egg in baking.

Textured Vegetable Protein (TVP)

This is a nutritious vegetarian supplement and is a great source of complete protein. It contains virtually no fat, and is a great source of iron, magnesium and phosphorus. Although it is technically a 'processed' food due to the process of defatting soy-flour, it is a great meat substitute and I use it on occasion. It comes packaged as 'dry granules'. Follow the packet instructions and soak in hot water, and you will see these granules absorb the water, producing a 'mince' consistency. I use TVP in recipes such as burger patties, meatballs and lasagne.

Gluten Flour

Wheat Gluten Flour is flour that has been treated so that the wheat bran and starch are removed. In this book, gluten flour is used to make mock meats such as seitan and vegan sausages. It cannot be substituted for regular flour or gluten-free options, so unfortunately, if you have a gluten intolerance, these recipes may not be the best for you.

Medjool Dates

I prefer to use Medjool dates in my recipes as they are a slightly 'meatier' date, are softer and break down easier when making bases for cakes or slices.

However, I am aware that the Medjool variety may not be easily available in certain areas or it may be quite expensive. If this is the case, I often substitute it with any variety of date, pit them if needed and soak them in boiling water for 30–45 minutes to soften them. Simply drain the liquid then use them in the recipe as normal. (Note that you may require more regular dates than if you were to use Medjools, as standard dried dates are a lot smaller!)

Sugar Substitutes and Sweeteners

You may notice a majority of my recipes call for some kind of sweetness (often in my savoury recipes as well as baking and raw desserts). My preferred sweetener of choice is coconut nectar, which is simply sap from a coconut tree. It is readily available in health food stores and online. It has a subtle caramel flavour and I don't find it too over-powering, plus it's full of vitamins, minerals and amino acids and doesn't cause crazy blood sugar spikes! It's a favourite of mine to add to savoury dishes as well – it really brings out the flavours and gives you the perfect balance of sweet and salty. I also regularly use organic maple syrup, rice malt syrup and coconut sugar or other forms of unrefined sugar. I personally have no fears around consuming sugar, and I enjoy it in abundance as I do live a very active lifestyle. If sugar is something you are trying to avoid, feel free to substitute with your sweetener of choice or adjust the quantities or omit. However, bear in mind some that forms of sweetener (i.e. stevia) are very overpowering so you don't need as much, and reducing or removing a sugar substitute in some recipes can alter the final outcome.

Oils

Many of my recipes call for different types of oil. Try and source organic, minimally processed brands. I do understand that many try to avoid consuming oil, so please feel free to substitute it out when frying by using a good, non-stick pan and a little water. However, reducing or removing oil in raw cakes and bakes can alter the final outcome, so please bear this in mind and find alternative substitutions instead of removing it altogether.

Vegetable Stock/Bouillon

A lot of my savoury recipes call for vegetable stock/bouillon. I find the addition of either of these takes flavours up a notch as opposed to just using regular table salt! I regularly interchange between using vegetable stock paste (page 200) or dehydrated stock (bouillon); I use the MSG-free kind and occasionally low-sodium varieties as well, so please feel free to either or omit completely to suit your taste preferences.

CHAPTER
1

BREAKFASTS

CACAO CRUNCH CEREAL
WITH CASHEW VANILLA CREAM

SERVES
« ··· 1–2 ··· »

For the cashew cream:
120g (1 cup) raw cashews,
    soaked for 3–6 hours
125ml (½ cup) coconut cream
80ml (⅓ cup) maple syrup
    or agave nectar
1 teaspoon pure vanilla
    extract with seeds
¼ teaspoon salt
2–3 tablespoons coconut oil

For the cereal:
90g (1 cup) wholegrain oats
40g (½ cup) coconut flakes
1 heaped tablespoon cacao
    powder
pinch of salt
180g or 9 large pitted
    Medjool dates
½ teaspoon vanilla powder
water, if needed

To serve:
plant-based milk of choice
1 banana, sliced
crushed nuts or seeds
    for some 'crunch'

These chewy, chocolatey and delicious morsels are such a fun way to eat breakfast! Pair them with your favourite nuts/seeds, some banana and a drizzle of delicious cashew cream.

A handy tip is to prepare the cereal the night before, and in the morning simply fill a bowl with the cereal and plant-based milk, some fruit and your favourite toppings!

1. Prepare the cashew cream first by blending the cream ingredients in a high powered blender until smooth and creamy and no lumps remain. Seal and store in the refrigerator until ready to use. Any leftovers can be stored in the refrigerator for 4–5 days.

2. To make the cereal, pulse the oats, coconut, cacao powder and salt in a high powered food processor until a crumb forms. Add the dates and vanilla and continue to process until a dough forms. Add a little water if needed.

3. Spoon into a bowl, wet your hands (to prevent sticking and to help it bind together) and gently begin to mould it further into a dough ball. Refrigerate for 10–15 minutes.

4. When ready to serve, roll the mixture into small, bite-sized balls/chunks. Serve with plant-based milk, banana, cashew cream and crushed nuts.

RAW COOKIE DOUGH CEREAL
WITH STRAWBERRIES & CHOCOLATE

SERVES
《··· 1–2 ···》

65g (½ cup) raw almonds
    or cashews (or a mixture
    of both)
90g (1 cup) wholegrain oats
180g or 9 large pitted
    Medjool dates
1 teaspoon vanilla powder
¼ teaspoon salt
water, if needed

To serve:
frozen or fresh strawberries
chopped vegan chocolate
plant-based milk of choice
fresh mint leaves (optional)

These little raw morsels are straight from the cookie gods. This recipe is super easy to prepare the night before, making a quick and easy breakfast option for the morning!

1. In a food processor or high-powered blender pulse the nuts and oats until a fine meal forms, add the dates, vanilla powder and salt, and keep pulsing until a dough forms. Add a little water if needed to help it bind together.

2. Roll into small balls, place into a bowl and refrigerate for around 10–15 minutes prior to serving.

3. Top with strawberries, chocolate and your desired amount of milk and enjoy.

PEANUT BUTTER JELLY
OVERNIGHT OATS

SERVES
《··· 1–2 ···》

250ml (1 cup) almond milk
125ml (½ cup) coconut milk
2 tablespoons smooth peanut
    butter, plus extra to serve
1 tablespoon coconut sugar
½ teaspoon vanilla powder
90g (1 cup) wholegrain oats
1 teaspoons chia seeds
2–3 tablespoons Raspberry
    & Chia Jam (page 198)

Once again, PB&J has my heart. I could probably bathe in the stuff.

This is a super delicious, quick and nutritious breakfast option. If you're in a rush, simply prepare it in a 'to-go' jar and eat it on the run!

1. Begin by blending the almond and coconut milk, peanut butter, coconut sugar and vanilla in a high speed blender until combined.

2. Pour the oats and chia seeds into a small bowl, and cover with the peanut butter milk – be sure to mix it well. The oats should be slightly covered by liquid.

3. Leave to soak overnight in the refrigerator.

4. In the morning, in your jar of choice, simply layer the oat mixture with a few spoonfuls of Raspberry & Chia Jam. Finish with a final dollop of peanut butter (optional). Enjoy!

BANOFFEE PIE
PORRIDGE PARFAIT

SERVES
《⋯ 1–2 ⋯》

For the crumble:
4 tablespoons raw almonds
4 tablespoons raw pecans
4 tablespoons coconut flakes
1 tablespoon coconut sugar
½ teaspoon ground cinnamon

For the banana-toffee layer:
2 ripe bananas
2–3 large Medjool dates, pitted
1 tablespoon coconut sugar
1 tablespoon almond butter
   or tahini
1 teaspoon pure vanilla
   extract with seeds
¼ teaspoon salt

For the porridge:
90g (1 cup) wholegrain oats
375–500ml (1½–2 cups)
   almond milk, plus more
   if needed
½ teaspoon pure vanilla
   extract with seeds
2 tablespoons maple syrup

For decorating:
1 ripe banana, sliced
black sesame seeds (optional)

Dessert takes breakfast. Or breakfast takes dessert. Either way, this is so sweet and delicious, and it is one of my favourite breakfasts in winter.

This recipe calls for a medium to large serving size – however you can easily split this recipe between two jars for a smaller portion to share with a loved one or family member. (Note – kids will love this!)

1. Prepare the crumble by pulsing the nuts, coconut, sugar and cinnamon in a food processor or blender until a fine crumb forms. Set aside.

2. Prepare your banana-toffee layer by blending the bananas, dates, coconut sugar, nut butter, vanilla and salt in a high speed blender or food processor until all lumps are gone. Set aside.

3. Prepare the oats by heating them in a small/medium saucepan with almond milk, vanilla and maple syrup over a medium heat until cooked (keep stirring to prevent the oats sticking to the pan). Adjust the liquid as necessary to reach your desired consistency.

4. Begin assembling the parfait by framing the bottom of a large glass jar with half of the banana slices.

5. Spoon half of the porridge into the jar, and gently top with a layer of caramel then a layer of crumble. Continue this procedure until you have used up all of the porridge and caramel.

6. Finish off with the remaining sliced banana and a sprinkle of sesame seeds, if you like.

NOTE: This could be split into two smaller jars.

COOKIE DOUGH OVERNIGHT OATS

SERVES

《··· 1 ···》

For the oats:
90g (1 cup) wholegrain oats
250ml (1 cup) almond, soy
    or cashew milk
125ml (½ cup) coconut milk
2 tablespoons maple syrup or
    coconut nectar (plus more
    if you like!)
1 teaspoon chia seeds or
    psyillium husk
1 teaspoon pure vanilla
    extract with seeds, or
    vanilla powder

**For the raw cookie dough
pieces:**
30g (⅓ cup) ground almonds
2 tablespoons almond butter
2 tablespoons maple syrup or
    rice malt syrup
1 tablespoon soft coconut
    butter
⅛ teaspoon salt
40g (¼ cup) chopped vegan
    chocolate of choice

I figured it was time to pimp up my regular overnight oats, and with my fascination with cookie dough, it was inevitable this was going to happen.

The small chunks of raw cookie dough are like little bites of heaven! Feel free to add any fruit or adjust the liquids and sweetness to suit your needs and desires.

Pictured on top of the jar and to the side are morsels of Cacao Crunch Cereal (page 22) which have been shaped into mini cookies.

1. In a medium bowl, prepare the oat mixture by combining all ingredients. The oats should be covered by around 1cm of liquid, so add more if necessary. Leave them covered in the refrigerator overnight.

2. In a small bowl, work the raw cookie ingredients with your hands until a soft dough forms. Also leave this covered in the refrigerator overnight.

3. In the morning, prepare your oats by breaking apart the raw cookie mixture with your hands and mixing it through the oats. Serve in a glass jar or a bowl and enjoy!

COCONUT AND VANILLA
RICE PUDDING

SERVES
⟪⋯ 1–2 ⋯⟫

100g (½ cup) short-grain rice
170ml (⅔ cup) coconut milk
  (plus more if needed)
2 tablespoons maple syrup
1 teaspoon vanilla powder
3 tablespoons sultanas or
  chopped dates
½ teaspoon ground
  cardamom
½ teaspoon ground cinnamon
pinch of nutmeg

To serve:
crushed pistachios
freeze-dried raspberries
drizzle of maple syrup or
  rice malt syrup

I actually love having rice for breakfast occasionally (I know, total weirdo – right?). However, it's super filling and it's essentially just porridge. Load this up with your favourite spices, toppings or anything you desire! Perfect for any time of the day.

1. Cook the short-grain rice following the package directions.

2. When the rice has nearly finished cooking (meaning there is still a tiny amount of liquid unabsorbed), add the coconut milk and reduce the heat to a simmer.

3. Add the maple syrup, vanilla, sultanas and spices and stir occasionally.

4. After around 3–4 minutes, remove the rice from the heat.

5. Stir in a little more coconut milk if you need to reach your desired consistency.

6. Serve in your favourite bowl and top with crushed pistachios, freeze-dried raspberries and a drizzle of maple syrup or rice malt syrup.

VANILLA CHAI PORRIDGE
WITH SALTED CARAMEL SAUCE

SERVES
《···1–2···》

For the oats:
4 tablespoons raw cashews
375ml (1½ cups) plant-based
    milk (oat, almond or soy)
1–2 teaspoons coconut sugar
    (or sweetener of choice)
1 teaspoon ground cinnamon
1 teaspoon ground cardamom
½ teaspoon ground cloves
1 teaspoon pure vanilla
    extract with seeds
90g (1 cup) wholegrain oats

For the salted caramel:
2 tablespoons hulled tahini
3 tablespoons maple syrup
¾ teaspoon salt

To serve:
1 ripe banana, sliced
2 tablespoons chilled
    coconut cream
ground cinnamon, for dusting
cinnamon sticks (optional)
vanilla pods (optional)
black sesame seeds (optional)

This breakfast is seriously a cuddle in a bowl. Chai spices are some of my favourites, and I was more than excited to incorporate them into my morning oats. I was even MORE excited to drown it in salted caramel sauce. And, I'm excited for you to try it. Feel free to adjust the liquid quantities to suit your 'porridge preferences'. C'mon, we all have 'em!

1. Begin by blending the cashews, plant-based milk, coconut sugar, spices and vanilla in a high-speed blender until smooth and creamy to form a 'chai' milk.

2. Heat the creamy chai milk with the oats in a small saucepan over a medium heat. Be sure to keep stirring until the oats have cooked (approximately 2–3 minutes). Adjust any liquids to reach your desired consistency.

3. Whisk the salted caramel ingredients together with a fork.

4. Pour the oats into your favourite bowl or dish and serve with sliced banana, coconut cream and a dusting of cinnamon. Drizzle the salted caramel over the top. Enjoy!

TURMERIC BAKED BEANS, POTATO HASH
& SAUTÉED GREENS

SERVES
≪··· 2 ···≫

For the potato hash:
3 medium-large potatoes,
    peeled and chopped
1 tablespoon vegan butter

For the baked beans:
2 teaspoons coconut oil
1 red onion, finely diced
1 garlic clove, minced
1 × 400g (14oz) can haricot
    (navy) beans, rinsed
    and drained*
1 teaspoon ground turmeric
1 teaspoon ground cumin
¼ teaspoon ground nutmeg
1 tablespoon coconut sugar
1–2 teaspoons vegetable
    bouillon or paste (page 200)
125ml (½ cup) tomato
    purée (paste)
½ × 400g (14oz) can chopped
    tomatoes
1 tablespoon coconut cream
salt and pepper, to taste

To serve:
sautéed (or raw) greens
    and mushrooms
hummus
sesame seeds (optional)
salt and pepper

* Feel free to substitute
    with any white beans.

Growing up in New Zealand meant that baked beans were going to be part of my DNA. I remember (quite regularly) having breakfast for dinner (AKA – beans on toast) many nights of the week. Sometimes, if I was lucky I would get the ones with the little sausages in it (if any New Zealanders are out there, you know what I'm talking about!).

Anyway – I wanted to take those baked beans and put a vegan spin on them, so here we have it!

Enjoy this heart-filling and belly-warming breakfast and revel in the anti-inflammatory and antioxidant benefits of turmeric alongside some delicious warming flavours.

1. Prepare the hash by chopping the potatoes and boiling until tender. Remove from heat and rinse in water.

2. In a non-stick frying pan simply fry the potatoes with the vegan butter over a medium heat until the potatoes are slightly crispy and broken up.

3. For the baked beans, heat up the coconut oil in a non-stick frying pan and sauté the onion and garlic until fragrant and browned.

4. Add the beans, spices, coconut sugar, vegetable stock, tomato purée and canned tomatoes. Simmer for 5–6 minutes over a medium heat.

5. Add the coconut cream and stir in. Remove from the heat and serve. Season to taste.

6. Serve the beans and potato hash with sautéed (or raw) greens and mushrooms of choice. Finish with hummus, sesame seeds and salt and pepper.

THE VEGAN BIG BREAKFAST

SERVES
《···1–2···》

For the hash browns:
3 medium–large potatoes,
    peeled and grated
2–3 tablespoons flour
    of choice
1 teaspoon onion powder
1 teaspoon garlic powder
1 teaspoon sea salt
oil, for frying

For the caramelised onion:
½ red or brown onion, cut
    into rings or strips
½ tablespoon coconut oil
salt, to taste
2 tablespoons coconut sugar

**For the garlic and herb
mushrooms:**
2 teaspoons vegan butter
4–5 button mushrooms,
    chopped in half
    (more if desired)
1 garlic clove, minced
1 teaspoon dried thyme
1 teaspoon dried rosemary
salt and pepper, to taste

To serve:
vegan sausages
    (store-bought or use
    my recipe on page 118)
smashed or sliced avocado
grilled tomatoes
spring onion (green
    onion), sliced

It's big, it's vegan and it's what's for breakfast.

1. Begin by turning your oven to a relatively low-medium temperature and place a lined baking tray inside.

2. To make the hash browns, place the grated potato in a large bowl and mix through the flour, onion and garlic powder and salt. Add more flour if needed until the mixture begins to stick together.

3. Shape into your desired 'hash brown' shape (I like to keep them quite thin so they cook faster and more efficiently). Fry the hash browns in a little oil in a non-stick frying pan over a low-medium heat for around 4–5 minutes on each side, until golden. Remove from the heat once cooked and transfer them to the lined baking tray in the oven, where you can keep them warm while you prepare the rest of the dish.

4. Lightly fry the onion in the coconut oil over a medium heat until the onion beings to sweat and soften. Add the coconut sugar and salt to taste, and increase the heat a little until the onion begins to caramelise. (Be careful not to burn.) Set aside.

5. To prepare the mushrooms, melt the vegan butter over a medium heat in a small saucepan, then add the mushrooms, garlic and herbs. Keep over this heat and continue to toss the mushrooms until they are well coated. Once the mushrooms begin to reduce in size, cover with a lid and remove from the heat until you are ready to serve.

6. Prepare any other components you would like to add to your breakfast. In this case, I simply fry my favourite brand of vegan sausage following the package instructions, slice and smash an avocado, grill some tomatoes and slice a spring onion (green onion). You could also add toast or some greens. Serve and enjoy!

BREAKFAST BURRITOS

2–3 large white or
    wholewheat wraps
2–3 tablespoons Sun-dried
    Tomato Pesto (page 186)
2 handfuls kale or spinach,
    de-stemmed and finely
    chopped
spring onion (green onion),
    finely chopped

For the potato hash:
3 potatoes, peeled if you like
2 vegan sausages, chopped
    into slices (store-bought or
    use my recipe on page 118)
1 tablespoon vegan butter
salt and pepper, to taste

For the tofu scramble:
coconut oil, for frying
170g (1½ cups) firm tofu,
    drained
1 teaspoon onion powder
1–2 teaspoons nutritional
    yeast
¼ teaspoon garlic powder
¼ teaspoon ground turmeric
¼ teaspoon ground cumin
60ml (¼ cup) plant-based
    milk
½ teaspoon cornflour or
    arrowroot flour
salt and pepper, to taste

These killer burritos are perfect for a weekend breakfast, brunch or even dinner.

Loaded with greens, potato hash, vegan sausage, tofu scramble and my favourite pesto – it's a flavour combo to die for! Feel free to add any vegetables or ingredients you like and supersize these burritos as much as you want.

1. Begin by chopping the potatoes for the hash into cubes. (You can leave the skin on or off.) Bring a saucepan of water to the boil and cook the potatoes until tender. Remove from the heat, drain, rinse them under cool water and drain again.

2. Prepare the hash by frying the potatoes and vegan sausage slices in a frying pan with a little vegan butter until golden and crispy. Season with salt and pepper and set aside.

3. Prepare the tofu scramble by heating coconut oil in a non-stick frying pan. Crumble the tofu with your hands into small pieces. Add the yeast, garlic powder, turmeric and cumin; and fry the tofu on a low-medium heat for around 1–2 minutes, breaking it apart with a fork.

4. Whisk together the plant-based milk and cornflour and add this to the pan. Stir until the mixture begins to thicken, then remove from the heat. Season to taste.

5. To assemble your wraps, begin by warming a wrap in the microwave for 10–20 seconds. Spread a layer of pesto in the centre of the wrap and assemble your components: kale, potato hash, tofu scramble and spring onion (green onion).

6. Fold the sides of the burrito in, then begin to fold it lengthways, ensuring you keep everything tightly packed. Follow the same procedure for the rest of the wraps. This recipe will yield 2 large wraps or 3 medium wraps, depending on how much of the filling you can squeeze into one!

CHAPTER
···· 2 ····

MAIN
MEALS

TERIYAKI 'CHICKEN' ON RICE
WITH CASHEW MAYO

SERVES
«··· 2 ···»

150–200g (¾–1 cup)
    sushi rice
2 tablespoons sushi vinegar

For the cashew mayo:
120g (1 cup) raw cashews,
    soaked for 3–6 hours
60ml (¼ cup) olive oil
125ml (½ cup) soy milk
1 tablespoon apple
    cider vinegar
½ teaspoon onion powder
1 tablespoon maple syrup
salt, to taste

For the teriyaki 'chicken':
1 × 560g (20oz) can young
    green jackfruit in water
    or brine
1 tablespoon coconut oil
½ brown onion, finely diced
80ml (⅓ cup) tamari
1 tablespoon mirin
3 tablespoons maple syrup
    or coconut nectar
1 teaspoon garlic powder
2 teaspoons onion powder
1 teaspoon toasted sesame oil
hot water, if needed

To serve:
sesame seeds
1 ripe avocado
pickled ginger

I ate teriyaki chicken (real chicken) with sushi and rice balls (if you've never had a rice ball, it's a ball of rice jam-packed with chicken, mayonnaise and avocado – life-changing stuff) like it was a religion when I was in my early teens. I recommend you get your hands on some jackfruit and make this teriyaki 'chicken' – it's so weirdly and amazingly close to the real thing, I have to pinch myself while eating it.

1. Prepare the sushi rice by following the packet instructions. Season with sushi vinegar and set aside to cool.

2. Prepare the cashew mayo by blending all of the ingredients in a high-powered blender until no lumps remain. Pour it into a sealable container or snap-lock bag and chill in the refrigerator whilst you make your 'chicken'.

3. Drain and rinse the jackfruit. Chop off the firm 'centre' so you are just left with the softer, sinewy edges.

4. Heat up the coconut oil in a medium frying pan and add the brown onion. Sauté until it is fragrant and slightly browned. Add the jackfruit, tamari, mirin, maple syrup, garlic powder, onion powder and sesame oil to the pan.

5. Simmer over a medium heat and slowly begin 'pulling' the jackfruit with a fork to break it apart. It will begin to resemble shredded chicken.

6. Simmer for around 4–5 minutes until soft, stirring occasionally. If it begins sticking to the pan, simply add a little hot water.

7. Serve over the sushi rice with a drizzle of the cashew mayo, sesame seeds, freshly sliced avocado and pickled ginger. Enjoy!

SPAGHETTI & 'MEAT' BALLS

SERVES
«··· 2–3 ···»

For the 'meat' balls:
135g (1½ cups) TVP mince
1 × 400g (14oz) can brown
    lentils, rinsed and drained
1 brown onion, finely diced
2 garlic cloves, minced
2 teaspoons light miso paste
½ teaspoon vegetable bouillon
    or paste (page 200)
1½ tablespoons coconut sugar
½ teaspoon ground nutmeg
½ teaspoons ground cloves
1 teaspoon smoked paprika
1–2 tablespoons flour of choice
1 tablespoon ground flaxseed
½ teaspoon salt
¼ teaspoon ground black pepper

For the sauce:
5–6 sun-dried tomatoes, drained
125ml (½ cup) salt-free tomato
    paste concentrate
1 × 400g (14oz) can chopped
    tomatoes
2 tablespoons maple syrup
    or coconut nectar
handful of basil leaves, plus
    extra to serve
2 teaspoons onion powder
1 teaspoon garlic powder
2 teaspoons dried rosemary
½ teaspoon ground nutmeg
½ teaspoon ground fennel
1 tablespoon vegetable stock
    paste (page 200)
¼ teaspoon ground black
    pepper

To serve:
250g spaghetti
vegan Parmesan (optional)

These 'meat' balls are so flavourful and super easy to make. The TVP (Textured Vegetable Protein) mince gives it a true, authentic mince-like texture – it's almost a little freaky. Paired with the delicious tomato and basil sauce, your favourite pasta and a sprinkle of vegan Parmesan – you are left with one impressive vegan dish that will fool the best of meat eaters.

1. Soak the TVP mince in water by following the packet instructions. Set aside.

2. In a high powered blender or food processor, blend the lentils, onion, garlic, miso paste, vegetable stock, coconut sugar and spices into a paste. Transfer to a large mixing bowl.

3. Once the TVP has absorbed all of the liquid, add this to the bowl. Mix in the flour and flaxseed until the mixture begins to bind together. Add a little more flour if necessary. Set aside for 10–15 minutes. In the meantime, preheat your oven to 190°C/375°F.

4. Roll the mixture into golf ball-sized balls and arrange neatly on a large baking tray lined with baking paper. Bake in the oven for 25–30 minutes, ensuring you flip them over halfway. Remove from the oven and allow to cool.

5. While they are cooling, prepare the sauce by blending all sauce ingredients in a high powered blender until smooth. Set aside.

6. Prepare your pasta of choice by following the packet instructions.

7. While the pasta is cooking, heat the coconut oil in a non-stick frying pan and then add the meatballs. Lightly fry for 1–2 minutes to allow the outer edges to crisp slightly, then add the sauce to the pan. Stir well until all of the meatballs are coated, stirring gently so they do not break apart. Heat for approximately 2–3 minutes.

8. Once your pasta is cooked, rinse and drain under cool water.

9. Serve the meatballs with the pasta, and finish with a few fresh basil leaves and vegan Parmesan (optional).

'BACON' & MUSHROOM CARBONARA

SERVES
≪··· 2 ···≫

250g (3 cups) fettuccine pasta
70g (1 cup) button or
    portobello mushrooms,
    finely diced
oil, for frying
parsley, to garnish

**For the quick and easy
coconut bacon:**
40g (½ cup) coconut flakes
3 tablespoons tamari
2 teaspoons liquid smoke
1 tablespoon maple syrup
1 teaspoon onion powder
1 teaspoon smoked paprika
1–2 teaspoons coconut oil

For the carbonara sauce:
120g (1 cup) raw cashews,
    soaked for 3–6 hours
½ teaspoon Dijon mustard
2 teaspoons onion powder
1 teaspoon garlic powder
¼ teaspoon ground nutmeg
½ tablespoon lemon juice
2 teaspoons maple syrup
375ml (1½ cups) soy, oat
    or almond milk
salt and pepper, to taste

This is one hell of a comforting dish! This was one of the first dishes I created when I became vegan and started sharing recipes, and it was a true favourite of mine but also of my friends and family! It's so creamy and delicious. Feel free to add any vegetables you like, or choose you favourite type of pasta if you're not a fan of fettuccine!

1. Cook your pasta following the packet instructions. Drain and rinse under cool water once cooked and set aside.

2. Prepare the coconut bacon by soaking the coconut flakes in the tamari, liquid smoke, maple syrup, onion powder and paprika for 5 minutes. Fry in a frying pan over a medium heat with a little coconut oil until only slightly crispy. Drain on a paper towel and set aside.

3. To prepare your sauce, simply blend the sauce ingredients in a high speed blender until thick and creamy. Set aside.

4. Heat a large frying pan and sauté the mushrooms in a little water or oil until tender. Add the cooked pasta to the pan and then toss through the sauce. Mix well until the pasta is evenly coated. Cook until the pasta is warm. Add more liquid to thin if desired.

5. Sprinkle the coconut 'bacon' on last, garnish with parsley and season with salt and pepper.

NOTE: When storing leftovers, keep them in an airtight container in the refrigerator. Heat up in a large pan using a little bit of soy, oat or almond milk to help thin out the sauce.

ULTIMATE VEGAN LASAGNE

SERVES
《··· 2–4 ···》

90g (1 cup) TVP (Textured Vegetable Protein)
2 garlic cloves, minced
1 brown onion, finely diced
1 tablespoon vegan butter or coconut oil
1 teaspoon ground nutmeg
1 teaspoon dried sage
1 teaspoon dried rosemary
1 tablespoon coconut sugar
2 teaspoons vegetable bouillon or paste (page 200)
80ml (⅓ cup) water, plus more if needed
700g (2¾ cups) passata
100g (1 cup) finely ground sunflower seeds or walnuts
8–9 instant lasagne sheets
200g (2 cups) grated vegan cheese
salt and pepper, to taste

For the bechamel:
2 tablespoons vegan margarine
2 tablespoons plain (all-purpose) flour
500ml (2 cups) plant-based milk
¼ teaspoon ground nutmeg
salt and pepper, to taste

The ULTIMATE comfort food – and you can rest assured and be comforted by the fact it's actually good for your soul! No animals were harmed in this lasagne, and boy – it honestly tastes like the real deal. If you are wanting to opt for a gluten-free option, simply use gluten-free lasagne sheets and a gluten-free flour in the bechamel. Enjoy!

1. Preheat your oven to 190°C/375°F.

2. Prepare the TVP by covering it with water in a bowl (follow the packet instructions) – this will allow it to expand into 'mince'.

3. In a large frying pan, brown the garlic and onion in either vegan butter or coconut oil.

4. Add the nutmeg, dried herbs, coconut sugar, stock powder or paste, water and TVP, and simmer over a medium heat for a further 2–3 minutes.

5. Add the passata and ground sunflower seeds or nuts. Reduce the heat and simmer for 3–4 minutes. Add more liquid if necessary. Season to taste. This is your 'meat' sauce.

6. Prepare the bechamel by melting the vegan margarine over a medium to high heat in a saucepan. Whisk in the flour until it forms a roux, then add 80ml (⅓ cup) of the milk. Continue whisking until a smooth paste forms, and slowly begin adding the rest of the milk, approximately 80ml (⅓ cup) at a time. Whisk after each addition until the sauce thickens before adding more milk. Add enough liquid to reach your desired consistency. Continue to cook in this way until the sauce coats the back of a spoon. You may not need all of the milk. Remove from the heat and season with nutmeg, salt and pepper.

7. Grab a 20cm×30cm (8×12 inch) deep baking dish and begin to assemble your lasagne. Start with a thin layer of the 'meat' sauce

followed by a layer of lasagne sheets. Ensure the lasagne sheets are evenly spaced, and that they are covered by sauce. Follow with another layer of 'meat' sauce, top with a layer of the bechamel sauce and then top with more lasagne sheets. Press down firmly each time you place the lasagne sheets on to help spread the sauce. Continue this method until you have added 5–6 layers of lasagne sheets. Occasionally I enjoy sprinkling some of the vegan cheese between the layers as well – however, this is totally optional. Top the lasagne with the remaining 'meat' sauce and bechamel, followed by the grated vegan cheese.

8. Cover with aluminium foil and bake in the oven for approximately 50–60 minutes until the lasagne is cooked through (use a knife to check). Remove the foil at the 40-minute mark and cook uncovered for the last 10–20 minutes.

9. Allow to stand for 15 minutes before slicing.

CHEESY MACARONI

SERVES
《··· 2–3 ···》

300g (4 cups) macaroni

For the sauce:
2 small potatoes, peeled
1 carrot
90g (¾ cup) raw cashews,
    soaked for 3–6 hours
40g (⅔ cup) nutritional
    yeast
500 ml (2 cups) soy milk or
    plant-based milk of choice
    (plus more if needed)
1 teaspoon arrowroot or
    cornstarch flour
1 teaspoon Dijon mustard
1 teaspoon white miso paste
1½ tablespoons maple syrup
    or rice malt syrup
1–2 teaspoons vegetable
    bouillon or paste
    (page 200)
2½ teaspoons onion powder
2 teaspoons garlic powder
¼ teaspoon white pepper
½ teaspoon smoked paprika
salt, to taste

This cheesy mac is super cheesy, not in the sense that it tells funny jokes (I mean – it may, I haven't bothered listening to what it has to say to be honest), but because nutritional yeast is the holy grail of vegan food. It will change your life. These magic flakes give this dish the most delicious, creamy and even cheesy flavour. Feel free to bump up your pasta's nutritional content by adding your favourite vegetables. Serve this with a side salad, some crusty bread or just eat it straight out of the pot (I promise you won't be judged).

1. Cook the pasta following the packet instructions. Rinse under cool water once 'al dente' and set aside in a large pot.

2. Roughly chop the potatoes and carrot and boil them in a small saucepan until tender. Drain and rinse under cool water.

3. Blend the potatoes and carrot with the rest of the sauce ingredients in a high-speed blender until thick and creamy and no lumps remain. Season to taste.

4. Pour the sauce into the pot with pasta, and heat over a medium-high heat for 3–4 minutes and ensure all the macaroni is well coated. If you like, feel free to thin the sauce out with more 'milk'.

5. Serve immediately with some salad, vegetables or crusty bread.

CREAMY POTATO BAKE

SERVES
《··· 2–3 ···》

6–7 large potatoes, peeled

For the sauce:
150g (1¼) cups raw cashews,
    soaked for 3–6 hours
220ml (¾ cup plus 2
    tablespoons) plant-based
    milk (almond, oat or soy)
190ml (¾ cup) thick coconut
    cream
2 tablespoons nutritional
    yeast
1 teaspoon onion powder
1 teaspoon garlic powder
2 teaspoons vegetable bouillon
    or paste (page 200)
2 teaspoons dried sage leaves
1 teaspoon dried thyme
½ teaspoon ground
    cardamom
½ teaspoon ground fennel
¼ teaspoon ground black
    pepper
50g (¼ cup) coconut sugar
1½ teaspoons cornflour
salt, to taste

To finish and garnish:
breadcrumbs of choice
    (opt for gluten-free for
    a sans gluten dish)
grated vegan cheese (optional)
balsamic glaze (store-bought
    is fine; choose one without
    preservatives)
parsley leaves

A lot of my cooking inspiration comes from my childhood. Potato bake being one of them. I have fond memories standing in my kitchen as a child eating the scraps in the pan, y'know. Those crusty remnants that cling on to the baking dish with dear life? Yeah. They taste super good.

However, traditional potato bake is laden with cream and butter, neither of which tend to leave you feeling the best. You see – I want you to feel good, but also not miss out on enjoying your 'creamy classics' while eating vegan. The secret ingredient here is the cashews, which give this potato bake the most amazing, creamy texture. Feel free to serve it up with salad or vegetables of your choice.

1. Slice the potatoes into thin rounds using a sharp knife or mandoline and set aside.

2. Blend all the sauce ingredients in a high-speed blender until all lumps are gone and it is thick and creamy.

3. Preheat your oven to 190°C/375°F.

4. In a deep ovenproof dish (I've used both a 20×20cm [8×8 inch] deep dish and a shallower 20×30cm [8×12 inch] dish – both have worked well), pour a small amount of the sauce evenly around the bottom of the dish and then arrange one layer of potatoes on the base, followed by a generous spread of the sauce. Continue with another potato layer and sauce layer. Press down firmly after each potato layer and continue with this method until you fill to the top of your dish. Cover with aluminium foil or a lid and bake, covered, in the oven for approximately 60–70 minutes until the potatoes are tender. (It may take more or less time depending how thinly you sliced your potatoes at step 1, so be sure to keep checking it!)

5. Sprinkle breadcrumbs or grated vegan cheese (or both) evenly over the top and bake for another 20–25 minutes until the top is golden and the potatoes are super soft.

6. Allow the potato bake to stand for at least 5–10 minutes before plating. Decorate with a drizzle of balsamic glaze and parsley leaves.

VEGAN BUTTER 'CHICKEN'
WITH NAAN

SERVES
2–3

200g (1 cup) basmati rice
300g (10½oz) seitan
(store-bought or use my
recipe on page 120)
1 tablespoon peanut oil
1 brown onion, finely diced
2 garlic cloves, minced
2 tablespoons vegan butter
2 bay leaves
2–3 teaspoons garam masala
1 teaspoon ground cumin
2 teaspoons freshly grated
ginger
½ teaspoon ground cinnamon
½ teaspoon ground turmeric
¼ teaspoon ground allspice
¼ teaspoon chilli powder (or
more if you prefer it hotter)
300ml (1¼ cups) vegetable
stock
salt, to taste

For the sauce:
120g (1 cup) raw cashews,
soaked for 3–6 hours
250g (1 cup) soy milk
125ml (½ cup) coconut cream
250ml (1 cup) reduced-salt
tomato paste
2 tablespoons coconut sugar
½ teaspoon arrowroot flour
or tapioca flour
2 teaspoons lemon juice

To serve:
warmed naan or roti bread

It honestly scares me how much this tastes like real Butter
Chicken. I used to eat my body weight in Butter Chicken before
turning vegan, and it's so refreshing to know I can still enjoy
this creamy and delicious curry without the cruelty. Feel free
to substitute the seitan with tofu, tempeh or chickpeas! Serve
it up with some naan and basmati rice and you have yourself
some awesome homemade take-out.

1. Cook the basmati rice following the packet instructions.
Keep it covered with a lid until ready to serve.

2. Begin by chopping the seitan (or tofu or tempeh) into bite-sized
pieces. Fry in the peanut oil until the outside is slightly golden and
crispy. Remove from the heat and place the pieces on a paper towel
to drain any excess oil. If you are using chickpeas, simply skip this
step and add them at step 3.

3. In a large frying pan, fry the onion and garlic in the vegan
butter until fragrant. Add the bay leaves and spices and stir-fry
for 2–3 minutes. Add the vegetable stock, season with salt and
reduce to a simmer.

4. While that is simmering, blend the rest of the sauce ingredients
(the cashews, soy milk etc) in a high-speed blender until smooth
and creamy and until all cashew lumps have been blended.

5. Add the seitan or vegan 'chicken' (or substitute) to the frying
pan with the spices and stock, and then add the creamy butter
chicken sauce you just blended. Stir well until everything is
combined. Simmer with the lid off for around 3–4 minutes until
the sauce has thickened. Feel free to then thin it out with a little
coconut milk or stock if you desire.

6. Serve your Butter 'Chicken' over basmati rice and with a side
of the naan or roti bread.

VEGAN FRIED 'CHICKEN' & GRAVY

For the fried vegan chicken
5 seitan cutlets (store-bought
    or use my recipe on page 120)
550–750ml (2–3 cups) oil, for
    frying (peanut, vegetable,
    canola or grape seed
    work best)

For the dry ingredients:
120 g (1 cup) plain
    (all-purpose) flour
1 teaspoon oregano
¼ teaspoon chilli powder
1 teaspoon dried sage
1 teaspoon dried basil
1 teaspoon dried marjoram
2 teaspoons paprika
1 teaspoon salt
1 teaspoon onion powder
1 teaspoon garlic powder
30g (¼ cup) cornstarch

For the batter:
2 flax eggs (2 tablespoons
    flaxseed mixed with
    6 tablespoons water and
    left to sit for 10 minutes)
250ml (1 cup) soy milk
2 teaspoons dark French mustard
3 tablespoons plain
    (all-purpose) flour
½ teaspoon cornflour
2 teaspoons vegetable stock
    powder
½ teaspoon ground black pepper
1 tablespoon vegetable
    stock powder

Okay, so hear me out – I get it, this is total comfort food. I definitely don't recommend you drown yourself in this everyday, but it's such a treat and makes for fun party food! If you are new to seitan, the texture can take some getting used to, essentially these resemble 'chicken nuggets'. Feel free to use any store-bought mock meat or my recipe on page 120. Alternatively, you can substitute with tofu and tempeh.

• •

To prepare the 'chicken':

1. Chop the seitan into bite-sized pieces. If using tofu or tempeh, cut into approximately 2-cm (3/4-inch) cubes. (For best results, prepare the seitan the evening before deep frying – this will avoid it becoming too soft.)

2. Blend the dry ingredients (except cornstarch) in a blender until combined, and set aside in a bowl. Blend the batter ingredients in a blender and set aside in another bowl.

3. Heat up the oil in a small or medium heavy pan until it reaches approximately 180–190°C (350–375°F).

4. Firstly, lightly coat the seitan cutlets in the cornstarch. Dip the mock meat into the batter, drip off any excess, then coat well with the dry ingredients.

5. Once your oil is hot enough, use a slotted spoon to place the cutlets (gently) in the oil. Only fry 1–2 cutlets at time – this will ensure the oil remains at a high temperature.

6. Deep fry for 2–3 minutes either side until golden.

7. Using a slotted spoon, gently remove from the oil and place onto a cooling rack with a paper towel placed underneath to drain any excess oil. Continue this process with all of the pieces until they are all cooked.

For the brown onion gravy:
2 brown onions, finely chopped
1 tablespoon vegan butter
1 teaspoon onion powder
1 teaspoon ground cumin
2 teaspoons muscovado sugar
1 tablespoon tamari
250g (1 cup) vegetable stock
2 teaspoons cornflour
hot water, to thin
salt and pepper, to taste

To prepare the gravy:

1. Brown the onions in a pan with the vegan butter until they begin to sweat and reduce in size by half.

2. Add the spices, sugar and tamari and sauté for a further 3–4 minutes. Add a little water to the pan to prevent sticking if needed.

3. Remove from the heat and allow to cool for around 3–4 minutes before blending.

4. Blend the onions with the vegetable stock and cornflour in a high-speed blender for around 3 minutes until silky smooth.

5. Heat in a small saucepan, thin with water if desired and serve immediately.

ULTIMATE BLACK BEAN NACHOS

SERVES
《··· 2–3 ···》

1 × 560g (20oz) can young
    green jackfruit in brine or
    water, rinsed and drained
1 tablespoon coconut oil
1 brown onion, finely diced
125ml (½ cup) salt-free
    tomato paste (purée)
125ml (½ cup) vegetable stock
2 teaspoons smoked paprika
2 teaspoons onion powder
1 teaspoon garlic powder
1 teaspoon ground cumin
½ teaspoon ground nutmeg
½ teaspoon chipotle
    chilli powder
½ teaspoon dried sage
2 tablespoons maple syrup
    or coconut nectar
1 tablespoon nutritional yeast
1 × 400g (14oz) can black
    beans, rinsed and drained
125ml (½ cup) extra
    water, if needed
    (to prevent sticking)

For the toppings:
corn chips
Cheesy Nacho Sauce
    (page 180)
Tomato & Mango Salsa (page
    176) or use store-bought
1 ripe avocado, sliced or
    mashed with salt, pepper,
    lime juice and coriander,
    to taste
fresh lime

These are killer. Well, they won't kill you – but seriously, killer. This is one of my favourite dishes (ever), and I'm so happy that I created it and am able share it with you. Go make it, now!

1. Prepare any toppings beforehand.

2. Slice the hard centre part away from the jackfruit chunks and discard, so you are just left with the softer sinewy edges (it will resemble shredded chicken).

3. In a non-stick frying pan, fry the onion in the coconut oil until fragrant. Add the tomato paste, vegetable stock, paprika, onion powder, garlic powder, spices, sage and jackfruit to the pan. Simmer over a low-medium heat for 4–5 minutes until some of the liquid has reduced. Using a fork, gently 'pull' away at the jackfruit – it will start to shred apart like shredded chicken.

4. Add the maple syrup, nutritional yeast and black beans to the pan. Add more water to the pan to prevent sticking if necessary. Remove from the heat after a few minutes and set aside.

5. Begin assembling your nachos by arranging corn chips on a plate. Top with the nacho 'meat', Cheesy Nacho Sauce (heat up as per recipe instructions on page 180), Tomato & Mango Salsa and avocado. Serve with fresh lime.

MEXICAN BAKED
SWEET POTATOES

SERVES
«···1–2···»

2–3 medium-large sweet
    potatoes
1 garlic clove, minced
1 tablespoon coconut oil
1 × 400g (14oz) can black
    beans, rinsed and drained
60g (½ cup) corn kernels
1 tablespoon tomato purée
    (paste)
1 teaspoon ground cumin
1 teaspoon paprika
½ teaspoon chilli powder
2 teaspoon onion powder
1 tablespoon coconut nectar
salt and pepper, to taste

To serve:
Cheesy Nacho Sauce
    (page 180)
coriander
fresh lime

I am a self-confessed sweet potato addict. I have a sweet potato
(or two, or three) EVERYDAY without fail. They are so versatile
and super easy to prepare – literally just pop it in the oven and
forget about it for an hour. You can fill it with your favourite sides
and toppings, and in this case I went full Tex-Mex because I love
Mexican food! These are great for a light lunch or dinner and
are simple to prep the night before work or school. Enjoy!

1. Begin by preheating your oven to 200°C/400°F. Wrap your
sweet potatoes in aluminium foil so that they are completely
covered. Bake in the oven for around 1 hour until they are soft.
(Baking time will vary depending on the size of your potatoes.)

2. Once the potatoes are nearly baked, in a non-stick frying pan
lightly fry the garlic clove in the oil until fragrant. Add the black
beans, corn, tomato purée (paste), spices, onion powder and
coconut sugar to the pan and fry for 3–4 minutes. Season to
taste. Remove from the heat.

3. Slit the potatoes down the centre and carefully fill them with
the black bean mixture. Reduce the heat of the oven and place
the potatoes back in to keep them warm while you prepare the
Cheesy Nacho Sauce according to the instructions on page 180.

4. To serve, simply cover your sweet potatoes in as much of the
hot nacho sauce as you wish! I used a squeeze bottle to achieve
the desired effect in the photo, but you could just spoon it on!
Finish with coriander and a squeeze of lime.

NOTE: Any leftover nacho sauce can be stored in an airtight container
in the fridge for up to 3–4 days. To re-use, simply thin it out with a little
soy or almond milk and reheat over a low-medium heat.

ONE-PAN MEXICAN RICE

SERVES
《···2–3···》

200–300g (1–1¾ cups) brown or white rice
250ml (1 cup) salt-reduced tomato paste
120g (1 cup) frozen corn kernels
1 × 400g (14 oz) can black beans, rinsed and drained
2 teaspoons vegetable bouillon or 2 tablespoons vegetable stock paste (page 200)
2–3 teaspoons smoked paprika
2–3 teaspoons ground cumin
2 teaspoons onion powder
1 teaspoon garlic powder
1–2 teaspoons ground chipotle chillies
1 tablespoon coconut sugar or coconut nectar
2 tablespoons nutritional yeast
salt and pepper, to taste
extra water, if needed

To serve:
coriander
corn chips (check that they are vegan)
fresh lime
Cheesy Nacho Sauce (page 180)

In a hurry and want minimal dishes to wash up? Then this is the meal for you!

Add any extra vegetables & beans if you wish to bulk it up for lunches or dinners.

This aromatic rice also can be used as a filling for burritos, nachos or quesadillas.

1. Cook the rice in a large saucepan by following the packet instructions.

2. Once the rice has absorbed all of the water, add the rest of the ingredients.

3. Keep stirring over a medium-high heat for around 3–4 minutes. Add some hot water, if needed, to adjust the consistency and prevent sticking.

4. Remove from the heat. Serve with coriander leaves, corn chips, fresh lime and a drizzle of Cheesy Nacho Sauce.

EASY PINEAPPLE FRIED RICE

SERVES
«···1–2···»

200g (1 cup) brown
    or white rice
2 tablespoons coconut oil
1 brown onion, finely diced
2 garlic cloves, minced
2 teaspoons grated ginger
120 (1 cup) frozen mixed
    vegetables of choice
1 × 375g (13 oz) can diced
    pineapple, rinsed
4–5 tablespoons tamari,
    plus more to taste
2 tablespoons mirin
2 tablespoons maple syrup
    or coconut nectar
1 teaspoon five-spice powder
1 teaspoon garam masala
200g (1¾ cups) firm tofu
½ teaspoon toasted sesame oil
salt and pepper, to taste

To serve:
white sesame seeds
coriander leaves

Super quick, easy and ultimately fool-proof. It's a great way
to use up any leftover rice if you have any as well!

1. Begin by preparing your rice by following the packet
instructions using your preferred cooking method. Set aside.

2. Heat the coconut oil in a large wok or frying pan and lightly fry
the onion, garlic and ginger until fragrant and slightly browned.

3. Add the frozen vegetables, pineapple, tamari, mirin, maple
syrup and spices and stir-fry for 2–3 minutes.

4. Add the cooked rice, and continue to stir-fry for another few
minutes. Season to taste.

5. Using your hands, crumble the tofu into the pan – then using
a fork lightly break it up and disperse it through the rice to give
it a 'scrambled egg' effect. Add the sesame oil last and season
with salt and pepper.

6. Remove from the heat and serve with a large sprinkle of white
sesame seeds and fresh coriander.

SWEET & SOUR TOFU

For the crispy tofu:
1 × 375g block firm tofu, drained
2–3 tablespoons cornflour
½ teaspoon salt
½ teaspoon onion powder
120g (1 cup) plain (all-purpose)
    flour
250ml (1 cup) soy milk
1 tablespoon apple cider vinegar
500–750ml (2–3 cups) vegetable
    oil, for deep frying

For the stir-fry:
2 garlic cloves, minced
2 teaspoons minced ginger
1 red (bell) pepper,
    finely chopped
110g (1 cup) cauliflower
1 × 300g (10½oz) can diced
    pineapple (drain and
    reserve the juice)
1 tablespoon coconut oil

For the sweet and sour sauce:
1 tablespoon tomato
    purée (paste)
60g (⅓ cup) raw cane sugar
80ml (⅓ cup) pineapple juice
60ml (¼ cup) rice vinegar
2 tablespoons tamari
2 teaspoons onion powder
1 teaspoon garam masala
1½ teaspoons cornflour

For the rice:
200g (1 cup) white basmati rice
juice of 1 lime
1 teaspoon toasted sesame oil
1 handful coriander leaves,
    roughly chopped
1 tablespoon black sesame seeds

My boyfriend and close friends love this recipe – I'm always getting begged to make it, so I thought I better share it here.

1. Cook the basmati rice by following the packet instructions. Once cooked, cover with a lid to keep warm and set aside.

2. Prepare the crispy tofu by firstly slicing the block of tofu into small cubes (around 2cm (¾ inch)). Dust in the cornflour and set aside.

3. Combine the salt, onion powder and flour in a bowl. In a separate bowl, whisk together the soy milk and apple cider vinegar until it begins to thicken. Add this to the flour, stirring until a batter forms.

4. Heat the oil in a saucepan until it reaches 190°C/375°F. Coat the dusted tofu cubes in batter and deep fry for 2–3 minutes on each side until golden. Remove from the hot oil and drain on a paper towel. Fry 1–2 cubes of tofu at a time to keep the oil temperature consistent.

5. Whisk together the ingredients for the sweet and sour sauce except for the cornflour. Set aside and prepare your vegetables for stir-frying, roughly breaking the cauliflower into pieces.

6. For the stir-fry, lightly fry the garlic, ginger, (bell) pepper, cauliflower and pineapple in the coconut oil for 3–4 minutes in a non-stick pan. Stir in the sweet and sour sauce and stir-fry for a further 3 minutes. Whisk the cornflour with 3 tablespoons of water and add this to the pan.

7. Once the sauce has thickened, stir through the tofu to coat and remove from the heat.

8. Add lime juice, sesame oil, coriander leaves and black sesame seeds to the pot of rice. Stir well and serve up.

LEMON HONEY TOFU

SERVES
≪⋯ 2 ⋯≫

For the crispy tofu:
250ml (1 cup) soy milk
2 tablespoons apple cider
vinegar
120g (1 cup) plain
(all-purpose) flour
½ teaspoon onion powder
½ teaspoon salt
500–750ml (2–3 cups) peanut
oil, for deep frying
40g (⅓ cup) cornflour
(plus more, if needed)
250g (2 cups) tofu, drained
and cut into 2 × 2cm chunks
(feel free to substitute with
tempeh or seitan)

For the lemon honey sauce:
125ml (½ cup) Vegan Honey
(page 185)
60ml (¼ cup) lemon juice
zest of 1 lemon
1 teaspoon toasted sesame oil
1½ tablespoons ketjap manis
(sweet soy sauce)
1–2 teaspoons onion powder
1 teaspoon garlic powder
¼ teaspoon chinese five spice
salt, to taste
1½ teaspoons cornflour
whisked with 2–3 teaspoon
water

To serve:
vegetables of choice (e.g.
broccoli, cauliflower etc.)
sesame seeds
rice noodles or basmati rice

Gooey, sticky, sweet and delicious! The crispy tofu is
devilishly good, so enjoy this as an option for a treat night
or 'home take-out' option! The great thing here is you are
in total control of what you are putting into your dish, unlike
when ordering take-out. Serve this up with rice, noodles
and your favourite vegetables.

1. To make the crispy tofu, whisk the soy milk and apple cider
vinegar in a bowl and let sit for a few minutes. Whisk in the flour,
onion powder and salt. Set up a dredging station to coat your tofu
(or substitute of choice)

2. Heat the oil (you want around 2–3 inches of oil) to 180–190°C/
350–375°F. Once the oil is hot enough you can begin deep frying.
Simply coat a piece of tofu in cornflour, then coat in the batter and
finish with a final coating of cornflour. Deep fry for approximately
1–2 minutes either side until golden brown. Remove using a
slotted spoon and transfer to a paper towel to drain any excess oil.
Deep fry 1–2 cubes at a time. Repeat this process for all pieces.

3. Prepare the Lemon Honey Sauce by whisking together the vegan
honey, lemon juice, lemon zest, toasted sesame oil, ketjap manis,
onion powder, garlic powder, five spice and salt.

4. Lightly stir-fry any vegetables of your choice in in a non-stick
frying pan with a little oil or a dash of water until tender.

5. Whisk the cornflour and water together and add this to the
pan, stirring continuously for a few minutes until the sauce
begins to thicken.

6. Add the crispy tofu to the pan and stir well for a further
1–2 minutes until all of the tofu is evenly coated in the sauce.

7. Serve over rice noodles or basmati rice and enjoy.

EASY FRIED NOODLES

SERVES
2

200g (2 cups) noodles
(flat rice or udon work
well; you can add more
noodles if you like)
vegetables of choice
(e.g. broccoli, mushrooms
and [bell] peppers)
1 tablespoon coconut or
vegetable oil
200g (1¾ cups) firm tofu,
drained and thinly sliced
or cubed

For the sauce:
2 garlic cloves, minced
60ml (¼ cup) tamari,
plus more to taste
juice of ½ lime
2 teaspoons grated ginger
1 teaspoon garam masala
1 teaspoon onion powder
½ teaspoon vegetable
stock powder
1 tablespoon coconut nectar
1–2 teaspoons toasted
sesame oil

To garnish:
coriander
sesame seeds

These noodles are perfect for those nights when you can't
really be bothered doing anything other than eating. It's
also one of those use-up-all-of-the-vegetables-in-the-fridge
recipes – y'know, those rogue, lonesome red peppers or
mushrooms? Yeah, those guys. They have a home right
here, amongst these noodles.

1. Begin by cooking your noodles following the packet
instructions. (For most rice noodle brands this requires
simply soaking in boiling water for 5–10 minutes.) Rinse
and drain your noodles once cooked and rinse under cold
water; this will stop them from cooking further and
sticking together.

2. Prepare your vegetables for frying by slicing them as
thinly or as small as you can and set aside.

3. Heat up a large wok or frying pan, add the coconut oil and
lightly fry the tofu and vegetables until the vegetables are
tender. Add a little water to the pan if they begin to stick.

4. Whisk together the sauce ingredients. Add the sauce and the
noodles to the pan. Mix well using tongs or a fork and continue
working the sauce through the noodles until well coated. Add
water as needed to prevent sticking.

5. Fry for around 3–4 minutes and then remove from the heat.

6. Serve with fresh coriander and sesame seeds.

EASY ONE-PAN
COCONUT CURRY

SERVES
2

200–300g (1–1¾ cups)
    jasmine rice (or more
    if desired)
2–3 large potatoes, peeled
1 × 400g (14 oz) can chickpeas,
    drained and rinsed
½ brown onion, finely diced
70g (1 cup) button
    mushrooms, finely diced
500ml (2 cups) coconut
    cream, plus more if you'd
    like it thinner
125ml (½ cup) vegetable stock
2–3 tablespoons maple syrup
1 teaspoon garam masala
2 teaspoons curry powder
1 teaspoon ground cardamom
1 teaspoon ground ginger
½ teaspoon ground nutmeg
½ teaspoon salt, plus more
    to taste
½ teaspoon ground black
    pepper
1–2 bay leaves

A quick, creamy and super fragrant curry for those lazy, after-work or school dinners.

1. Cook your desired amount of jasmine rice following the packet instructions. At the same time in a separate saucepan, chop the potatoes into cubes and boil until tender. Set aside.

2. In a large frying pan, fry the chickpeas and onion in a little oil until the onion begins to sweat.

3. Add the rest of the ingredients to the pan and leave to simmer on a medium heat for 10 minutes, stirring occasionally. Finally, add the potatoes and stir in.

4. Remove from the heat allow to cool for 2–3 minutes before serving.

5. Serve on a bed of jasmine rice and enjoy.

NOTE: You can add more or use less coconut cream to reach your desired consistency. The curry will reduce once you let it sit, so I like to add a little coconut cream just before I serve it.

MOROCCAN CHICKPEA & AUBERGINE CURRY

200–300g (1–1¾ cups)
  rice of choice
1 tablespoon coconut oil
1 red onion, finely diced
2 garlic cloves, minced
70g (1 cup) aubergine
  (eggplant), diced
2 teaspoons cumin seeds
2 teaspoons ras el hanout
2 teaspoons sweet paprika
1 teaspoon ground turmeric
1 teaspoon ground nutmeg
2 teaspoons onion powder
1 teaspoon ground fennel
2 tablespoons tomato
  purée (paste)
60ml (¼ cup) vegetable stock
2 tablespoons coconut sugar
  or nectar
1 × 400g (14oz) can chickpeas,
  rinsed and drained
250ml (1 cup) coconut cream
salt and pepper, to taste

To serve:
Oil-free Hummus (page 183)
leafy greens of choice
seeds or nuts of choice

This is, hands down, one of my favourite curries! It's full of bold and earthy flavours. Feel free to add any vegetables and serve it over rice or potatoes. Try adding some hummus and leafy greens to create a colourful and nutritious dish. This is great to make in bulk and refrigerate ahead of time, and is easy to reheat – perfect for meal prepping or for those nights when you are pressed for time.

1. Begin by cooking your desired rice of choice following the packet instructions. I prefer a mix of brown and wild rice.

2. Melt the coconut oil in a large frying pan and add the onion, garlic and cumin seeds. Fry these over a medium heat until fragrant. Add the diced aubergine (eggplant), spices, onion powder, ground fennel and tomato purée (paste) and cook for 3–4 minutes until the aubergine (eggplant) begins to soften. Add water if needed to prevent sticking.

3. Add the vegetable stock, coconut sugar and chickpeas and simmer for 5–10 minutes, stirring occasionally.

4. Add the coconut cream. Stir well, cover the pan with a lid and leave to simmer on a low heat for around 5 minutes.

5. To serve, plate up your cooked rice and a serving of the curry followed by some hummus, leafy greens and a sprinkling of seeds.

RUSTIC LENTIL DHAL

2–3 potatoes, peeled
1 tablespoon vegan butter
    or coconut oil
1 brown onion, finely diced
2 garlic cloves, minced
2 teaspoons grated ginger
2 teaspoons ground cumin
2 teaspoons garam masala
2 teaspoons ground turmeric
1 teaspoon ground coriander
1 teaspoon ground cardamom
½ teaspoon chilli powder
½ teaspoon ground cinnamon
2 bay leaves
1 tablespoon coconut sugar
125ml (½ cup) vegetable stock
60g (½ cup) frozen corn
    kernels
2 × 400g (14oz) cans brown
    lentils, rinsed and drained
1 × 400ml (14fl oz) can
    coconut cream
200g–400g (1–2 cups)
    basmati rice (or more
    if desired)

This is a little different than your traditional dhal, mainly because I use canned lentils instead of uncooked ones. Basically, I'm lazy sometimes and I prefer the canned variety! Always choose organic and low sodium versions when using canned beans, and always, and I mean ALWAYS, rinse them well under water before adding them to your dish. All fart jokes aside – this dish is delicious and easy to make.

1. Roughly chop the potatoes into small cubes (approximately 2cm/ ¾ inch). Bring a medium saucepan of water to the boil and boil the potatoes until tender. Remove from the heat and rinse under cool water. Set aside.

2. Heat the vegan butter or coconut oil in a large frying pan and fry the onion and garlic until fragrant. Add the ginger, spices, bay leaves, coconut sugar and vegetable stock and simmer, covered, for 5 minutes, stirring occasionally.

3. Add the potatoes, corn, lentils and coconut cream and simmer uncovered for around 3–4 minutes. Adjust the consistency by adding more coconut cream if preferred.

4. While this is simmering, cook your basmati rice following the packet instructions.

5. Allow the dhal to sit for 5 minutes before serving.

PUMPKIN & COCONUT RISOTTO

《⋯ 2 ⋯》

1 brown onion, finely diced
2 garlic cloves, minced
1 tablespoon vegan butter
300g (1½ cups) arborio rice
1 tablespoon coconut sugar
1 teaspoon ground cardamom
¼ teaspoon ground nutmeg
½ teaspoon garlic powder
½ teaspoon ground fennel
625ml (2½ cups) vegetable
    stock
250ml (1 cup) pumpkin purée
1 × 400ml (14 fl oz) can
    coconut cream
salt and pepper, to taste

To serve:
splash of coconut cream
    or plant-based milk
black sesame seeds
fresh basil

This is one of my favourite ways to enjoy pumpkin! This dish is both creamy and delicious. If you're like me, it won't even make it to the plate and you'll be left eating it out of the pan.

1. In a large non-stick frying pan, sauté the onion and garlic in vegan butter until fragrant.

2. Add the uncooked rice, sugar, garlic powder and ground fennel and sauté for another minute to seal the rice.

3. Over a medium heat, slowly add the vegetable stock to the pan 80ml (⅓ cup) at a time, ensuring you stir well to prevent sticking, and wait until the liquid has been absorbed by the rice before you add the next lot of stock.

4. Once all of the stock has been absorbed, add the pumpkin purée and coconut cream. Reduce the heat slightly to a moderate simmer and simmer uncovered for 5–6 minutes until the rice is al dente and some of the liquid has been absorbed. Add more coconut cream or plant-based milk if you'd like or if you need to adjust the consistency. Garnish with fresh basil.

PUMPKIN FLATBREAD

SERVES
《⋯ 1–2 ⋯》

For the flatbread:
130g (1 cup) plain
    (all-purpose) flour
65g (⅓ cup) pumpkin purée
3 tablespoons coconut yogurt
1 teaspoon onion powder
½ teaspoon ground cumin
½ teaspoon sea salt
1 tablespoon melted
    vegan butter

Topping options:
Aioli (page 189)
Walnut & Kale Pesto
    (page 190)
1 large, ripe avocado, smashed
leafy greens
sliced cherry tomatos
black sesame seeds
salt and pepper, to taste

Sometimes you want something a little fancier than toast or a sandwich, and I'm pleased to say – this flatbread is your guy! Made from simple ingredients that are easily found in the kitchen and taking less than 20 minutes to make, it's safe to say your lunch or brunch is going to be great. Please also note that this flatbread is totally customisable! I encourage you to explore your creativity in the kitchen, so please feel free to experiment with your favourite toppings, such as pesto, nut butter, vegan cheese or hummus.

1. Preheat your oven to 200°C/400°F.

2. In a large mixing bowl, mix the flour, purée, coconut yogurt, onion powder, cumin and salt together until a dough ball forms. Add a little more flour if the dough is sticking. Roll it out onto a floured surface and knead for 1–2 minutes. Dust a rolling pin with flour to prevent it sticking and roll the flatbread out into your desired shape and thickness. Poke holes in the flatbread with a fork to prevent it rising.

3. Brush with the melted vegan butter and bake in the preheated oven for 10–12 minutes until the edges begin to crisp.

4. Prepare your favourite toppings and top as desired. Pictured is a generous spread of smashed avocado, followed by tomatoes, leafy greens, Aioli, black sesame seeds and salt and pepper to taste.

MAPLE FRIED TOFU SPRING ROLLS
WITH PEANUT AND GINGER DIPPING SAUCE

SERVES
《··· 8–10 ···》
OR MORE

For the rice paper rolls:
200–250g (1¾–2 cups)
    firm tofu, cut into thin
    strips (around 0.3-cm/
    ⅛-inch thick)
2 tablespoons tamari
3–4 tablespoons maple syrup
¼ teaspoon onion powder
½ teaspoon toasted sesame oil
1 tablespoon coconut oil
100–200g (2–4 cups)
    vermicelli noodles
1 × packet rice paper sheets
1 large ripe avocado, sliced
finely shredded vegetables
    (I use courgette, carrot
    and red cabbage)
pickled ginger

**For the sweet peanut and
ginger dipping sauce:**
3 heaped tablespoons
    peanut butter
1 heaped tablespoon
    grated ginger
80ml (⅓ cup) maple syrup
80ml (⅓ cup) coconut milk
1 teaspoon miso paste
½ teaspoon onion powder
1 tablespoon lemon juice
hot water, if needed
salt, to taste

These rolls are my go-to for a light lunch, snack or dinner. I think the thing I like the most about these is that you really can customise them to suit your taste preferences – you can fill the rice paper with anything you fancy! The success with these rolls all comes down to the assembly – rice paper can be a tricky medium to work with (it's sticky and thin), but after a few goes you'll be rolling away with success. The key here is having a clean work station and a wet tea towel or dish cloth to roll on, to prevent any possible tearing and sticking.

1. Begin by marinating your tofu strips in the tamari, maple syrup, onion powder and sesame oil for at least 30 minutes.

2. Heat the coconut oil in a large, non-stick frying pan and fry the tofu strips for 3–4 minutes, flipping halfway so that both sides become crispy. Drain on a paper towel and set aside.

3. Soak your vermicelli noodles in boiling water for 5 minutes, then drain and rinse with cool water. Set aside in a bowl.

4. Now, the most efficient way I find to assemble my rice paper rolls is firstly setting up a 'work station'. This involves preparing all the fillings that you want in your rice paper rolls (I like to set them out in front of me in separate bowls) and laying out a large chopping board. Cover the chopping board with a wet tea towel or dish cloth. Nearby, keep a large pot or frying pan filled with 5cm/2 inches hot water (you will be dunking the rice paper in here, so make sure it is large enough to fit the circumference of one rice paper sheet). I also like to work near the kitchen sink, as it can get quite messy! With all that in order, you can begin rolling! Grease the plate you are planning to serve them on to prevent any sticking.

5. Start by placing a rice paper sheet in the hot water for a few seconds, completely submerging it. Transfer it to the wet cloth.

6. Place a slice of tofu in the centre and gently lay your desired ingredients around and on top of the tofu. Be sure to keep everything tightly packed in the centre. I use a pinch of noodles, a few slices of avocado, a pinch of vegetable mix and some slices of pickled ginger for each one.

7. Rolling the rice paper rolls takes practice – the first couple may rip. If this does happen, you can just double-roll them, so do not stress. Begin by taking the edge that is closest to you, pull it over the ingredients and begin rolling away from you. As you roll, keep the mixture tight, and at the same time fold in each separate end (left and right) – you are essentially rolling a very small burrito.

8. Ensure all ends are tucked in and place them on a greased serving plate. Pop them in the refrigerator until you are ready to serve. Repeat the above steps until you have run out of mixture.

9. To prepare the dipping sauce, simply blend in a high speed blender. Thin with hot water if desired and add salt to taste.

10. Dip your spring rolls in the dipping sauce, and serve!

• •

NOTE: Double dipping is totally acceptable and, if anything, completely necessary.

LOADED VEGAN HOT DOGS

SERVES
2–3
DOUBLE FOR MORE

For the sweet chilli sauce:
1–2 teaspoons hot sauce
    or chilli paste
2 tablespoons reduced-salt
    tomato purée (paste)
2–3 tablespoons maple syrup
1 teaspoon garlic powder
1 teaspoon onion powder
½ teaspoon salt
water to thin, if necessary

For the cheesy mustard mayo:
1 teaspoon Dijon mustard
1 tablespoon tahini
1 tablespoon maple syrup
2 teaspoons nutritional yeast
1 teaspoon onion powder
3–4 tablespoons hot water
    (to reach your desired
    consistency)
⅛ teaspoon salt

For the hot dogs:
2–3 vegan sausages
    (either store-bought or
    use my recipe on page 118)
½ red onion, sliced
1–2 tablespoons oil, for frying
2–3 hot dog buns
salt and pepper, to taste
sesame seeds

These babies are super simple, delicious and great for kids and adults alike.

Feel free to add any of your favourite sauces and toppings to create your ultimate hot dog!

I like to use my own vegan sausage recipe. However, if you are pressed for time, any store-bought variety will do.

1. Prepare the sauces by mixing each separately in a bowl and storing in resealable plastic bags. Set aside.

2. In a large frying pan, fry the vegan sausages and red onion in a little oil until the sausage is browned and crispy on all sides and the onion is crispy. Drain both on a paper towel.

3. Warm the buns in the oven or microwave.

4. To assemble the hot dogs, cut a slice down the centre of the hot dog bun with a bread knife (ensure you do not cut all the way through). Spread a thin layer of sweet chilli sauce inside the bun and then insert the vegan sausage. Top with onion, salt and pepper and finish with a drizzle of both the sweet chilli sauce and cheesy mustard mayo. (To apply the sauces, simply slice a small corner off the resealable plastic bags with scissors and squeeze as you would with a piping bag.) Sprinkle with sesame seeds.

5. Feel free to add any additional toppings to your hot dogs, such as grated vegan cheese or pickles!

VEGAN SAUSAGE ROLLS

MAKES

《⋯ 9–12 ⋯》

2–3 sheets frozen puff pastry

2 × 400g (14oz) cans lentils, rinsed and drained

1 tablespoon vegan butter

1 brown onion, finely chopped

2 garlic cloves, minced

200g (3 cups) very finely diced button mushrooms

2 teaspoons ground cumin

1 teaspoon garam masala

½ teaspoon ground nutmeg

½ teaspoon ground fennel

1 teaspoon dried sage

1 tablespoon tamari

2 teaspoons vegetable bouillon or paste (page 200)

2 teaspoons ground flaxseed

1–2 tablespoons almond milk, for brushing

1–2 tablespoons sesame seeds, for decoration

The perfect party snack! Kids will love making these, and so will you. These take me back to my childhood parties. It was either a combination of sausage rolls and fairy bread – one of the two made me throw up at the majority of my birthdays. (If you don't know, fairy bread is white bread filled with butter and hundreds and thousands. Clearly something a fairy would eat, right?)

Well, you need not worry about feeling sick or tired from these – no sausage is to be seen, just lots of beans, vegetables and delicious flavours.

1. Remove the puff pastry sheets from the freezer to allow them to partially thaw. You want them just pliable, so put them in the fridge if you won't use them for a while.

2. Preheat your oven to 190°C/375°F.

3. Pulse the lentils in a food processor until they form a purée. (Don't make it completely smooth – you want a few whole lentils lingering around.)

4. Heat the vegan butter in a large frying pan and sauté the onion and garlic until fragrant. Add the button mushrooms to the pan and along with the spices, ground fennel, sage, tamari and bouillon. Sauté for 1–2 minutes until the mushrooms begin to sweat.

5. Add the lentil purée to the pan. Sauté for a further 1–2 minutes. Remove from the heat, stir in the ground flaxseed and set aside.

6. Lay out your puff pastry on a large working space. Cut each puff pastry sheet in half widthways so you have 4–6 long rectangles.

7. Working with one rectangle at a time, spoon approximately 2–3 heaped tablespoons of mixture down the centre, forming a long, even 'sausage' shape. Shape it with your hands if you need.

8. Brush the edges with a little almond milk, and then roll the pastry up, enclosing the filling. Ensure the 'seam side' is facing down. Cut into 4–5 sections using a pastry cutter or a sharp knife (depending

what size you'd like your rolls) and transfer them to a baking sheet lined with parchment paper. Arrange them with around 1–2 cm (½– ¾ inch) between each roll.

9. Brush each roll with almond milk and then sprinkle some sesame seeds on top.

10. Follow the procedure with the rest of the rolls and then bake for around 20–30 minutes, or until your puff pastry has puffed up and is golden!

· ·

PUFF PASTRY TIPS: Ensure that you work with the puff pastry relatively quickly once it has defrosted and is just pliable – this will ensure you don't have any mishaps with it rising. If the pastry is at room temperature it will become soggy and floppy – not really what you want in a sausage roll!

LENTIL BOLOGNESE

SERVES
《··· 2–3 ···》

1 brown onion, finely diced
2 garlic cloves, minced
1–2 tablespoons vegan butter
70g (1 cup) button
    mushrooms, finely diced
40g (½ cup) aubergine
    (eggplant), finely diced
250ml (1 cup) salt-reduced
    tomato paste
125ml (½ cup) vegetable
    stock, plus more if needed
1 teaspoon dried sage
1 teaspoon dried thyme
½ teaspoon dried oregano
2 teaspoons smoked paprika
1 teaspoon ground nutmeg
½ teaspoon ground cloves
1 tablespoon nutritional yeast
1½ tablespoons coconut sugar
2 × 400g (14oz) cans brown
    lentils, rinsed and drained
salt and pepper, to taste
250–300g wholemeal
    spaghetti

To serve:
chopped spring onion
    (green onion)
hemp seeds

This is one of my favourite weeknight meals, because it's so quick, easy to make, super flavourful and good for your body and soul. Feel free to bump it up with any of your favourite vegetables.

1. Brown the onion and garlic with the vegan butter in a large saucepan until fragrant.

2. Add the mushrooms, aubergine, tomato paste, stock, herbs and spices and simmer on a medium heat for 3–4 minutes.

3. Add the nutritional yeast, coconut sugar and brown lentils and simmer for another 5–6 minutes until the sauce has reduced. Add a little more water if it becomes too thick or sticks to the pan. Season to taste.

4. Remove from the heat and cover with a lid. In a separate pan, cook your pasta following the packet instructions.

5. Rinse and drain the pasta under cool water once cooked.

6. Serve the bolognese with pasta and finish with chopped spring onion and hemp seeds.

SHEPHERD'S PIE

SERVES
≪⋯ 2 – 3 ⋯≫

For the potato topping:
1 large sweet potato, peeled
2 potatoes, peeled
1 tablespoon vegan butter
½ teaspoon ground nutmeg
salt and pepper, to taste
light spray of olive oil
coriander, to garnish

For the lentil and vegetable filling:
1 brown onion, finely diced
2 garlic cloves, minced
coconut oil, for frying
1 tablespoon vegetable bouillon
    or paste (page 200)
1 teaspoon dried sage
½ teaspoon dried thyme
½ teaspoon ground nutmeg
½ teaspoon ground cloves
1 tablespoon coconut sugar
1 teaspoon blackstrap
    molasses or black treacle
30g (½ cup) button
    mushrooms, finely diced
50g (½ cup) mixed frozen
    vegetables
2 × 400g (14oz) cans brown
    lentils, rinsed and drained
2 tablespoons cornflour
125ml (½ cup) plant-based
    milk (oat, rice, almond
    or soy)

This is one heck of a heart-warming, wintry meal that you and your nearest and dearest will love! It's super easy to make and packed full of protein and good carbohydrates, all of which your body will thank you for.

1. Preheat your oven to 190°C/375°F.

2. Chop the sweet potato and regular potatoes into even-sized chunks. Cook in a saucepan of boiling water for about 10 minutes until soft.

3. Meanwhile, for the filling, lightly fry the onion and garlic in water or oil until fragrant. Add the bouillon, herbs and spices, coconut sugar, molasses, mushrooms, vegetables and lentils. Stir well and sauté for 2–3 minutes until the vegetables have defrosted.

4. Whisk together the cornflour and plant-based milk of your choice and add to the pan. Keep over the heat until the mixture begins to thicken. Once thickened, remove from the heat.

5. Remove the potatoes from the heat and drain under cool water. Add them back to the pot and mash with the vegan butter, nutmeg and salt and pepper to taste.

6. Evenly distribute the lentil and vegetable mixture in a deep 20×20 cm (8×8 inch) baking dish. Top with the mashed potatoes and lightly spray with olive oil.

7. Bake in the preheated oven for 15–20 minutes until the top is slightly golden and crispy. Allow to rest for 5 minutes prior to serving.

VEGAN SOUVLAKI
(GYROS/KEBAB)

MAKES
《··· 3–4 ···》
SOUVLAKI

For the tabbouleh:
70g (½ cup) pearl couscous
    or bulgur wheat
2 handfuls parsley, finely
    chopped
½ red onion, finely chopped
2 handfuls mint leaves,
    finely chopped
juice of 1 lemon
1 tablespoon olive oil
salt and pepper, to taste

For the coconut and mint yogurt:
120g (1 cup) raw cashews,
    soaked for 3–6 hours
175ml (⅔ cup) coconut cream
1 tablespoon maple syrup
    or rice malt syrup
1 tablespoon lemon juice
1½ tablespoons apple cider
    vinegar
2 handfuls mint leaves
1 handful coriander leaves
1 tablespoon olive oil
salt and pepper, to taste

For the falafel:
1 × 400g (14oz) can chickpeas,
    rinsed and drained
2 handfuls of roughly
    chopped kale
1 handful chopped parsley
2 garlic cloves
2 teaspoons onion powder
2 teaspoons ground cumin
2 teaspoons ground coriander

This recipe does require a little more preparation than most of the recipes in this book, but it is WELL worth the extra effort. The combinations of flavours are insane, and it's seriously so delicious. If you can't find jackfruit, you can leave it out, but it takes this dish to another level so I'd recommend checking out your local Asian grocery store, or order online. Please ensure it is the 'young green' variety too.

1. Prepare the tabbouleh first by cooking the couscous or wheat following the packet instructions. Drain and rinse under cool water and mix together with the parsley, onion, mint, lemon, olive oil and salt and pepper. Set aside.

2. Prepare the coconut and mint yogurt by blending all the ingredients in a high-speed blender. Set aside in the refrigerator until ready to use. (I like to prepare this while the wheat or couscous is boiling.)

3. Start to make the falafel. Simply process all the ingredients except for the flour and frying oil in a food processor or high-speed blender until smooth. Transfer to a large bowl and mix through the flour until a dough forms. Add more flour if the mixture is too sticky.

4. Roll the falafel into golf ball-sized balls and gently press down with your hands to flatten them slightly. Lightly fry the patties in a frying pan over a medium-low heat in oil for around 4 minutes both sides until golden and crispy. Remove from the heat and cover with a lid until ready to use.

1 heaped tablespoon tahini

1 teaspoon vegetable bouillon or paste (page 200)

1 tablespoon maple syrup or coconut nectar

juice of 1 lemon

2 tablespoons olive oil

3 tablespoons plain (all-purpose) flour (more if needed)

salt and pepper, to taste

1–2 tablespoon oil, for frying

For the souvlaki 'meat':

1 × 560g (20oz) can of young green jackfruit (in water or brine)

1 garlic clove, minced

1 brown onion, finely sliced

1 tablespoon grapeseed oil

2 tablespoons coconut nectar

1 tablespoon tamari

2 teaspoon onion powder

1 teaspoon garlic powder

1–2 teaspoons dried oregano

½ teaspoon ground sage

1–2 teaspoons lemon juice

80ml (⅓ cup) vegetable stock, plus extra water as needed

salt and pepper, to taste

To serve:

Lebanese bread

hummus

5. To prepare the souvlaki 'meat', drain the jackfruit and rinse under water. Pull the sinewy ends of the fruit away from the solid centres (discard the centres). It will resemble shredded meat.

6. Fry the onion and garlic over a medium heat in oil until fragrant. Add the coconut nectar, tamari, onion powder, garlic powder, sage, lemon juice and jackfruit to the pan. Gently 'pull' at the jackfruit with a fork and break it into smaller pieces. Add the vegetable stock and simmer for 4-5 minutes, adding more liquid as necessary to prevent sticking. Once most of the liquid has been absorbed and the jackfruit has softened and is well shredded, simply remove from the heat. Season to taste.

7. To assemble your souvlaki, warm up the Lebanese bread in a hot pan. Transfer it to a flat surface and spread a thick layer of hummus in the centre, followed by a generous serving of tabbouleh, some falafel (I chose to break my falafel into small chunks), some shredded jackfruit 'meat' and finish with coconut mint yogurt. Fold the bottom of the souvlaki up and fold the sides in to create a 'pocket' – secure it in foil, parchment paper or in a paper bag to stop the bottom from leaking.

8. Follow this procedure for the remaining ingredients and serve.

TEX MEX PIZZA

MAKES
1
LARGE PIZZA

For the pizza dough:
240g (2 cups) plain
    (all-purpose) flour
½ teaspoon salt
1 teaspoon cumin
½ teaspoon paprika
1 tablespoon raw cane sugar
1 tablespoon instant dry yeast
170ml (⅔ cup plus 2 tablespoons)
    warm water

For the sweet chilli sauce:
1–2 teaspoons hot sauce
    or chilli paste
2 tablespoons reduced-salt
    tomato purée or paste
2–3 tablespoons maple syrup
1 teaspoon garlic powder
1 teaspoon onion powder
½ teaspoon salt
water, to thin if necessary

For the Tex-Mex bean mix:
½ red onion, finely chopped
2 garlic cloves, finely chopped
1 tablespoon coconut oil
1 × 400g (14oz) can of black beans,
    rinsed and drained
60g (½ cup) frozen corn kernels
1 teaspoon vegetable stock powder
2 teaspoons coconut sugar or
    coconut nectar
1 teaspoon ground cumin
½ teaspoon ground coriander
½ teaspoon paprika
salt and pepper, to taste

For the toppings:
90–135g (1–1½ cups) grated
    vegan cheese (brand of choice)
1 yellow (bell) pepper, thinly sliced
6–8 cherry tomatoes, halved
Cashew Mayo (page 44)
coriander leaves to garnish

The perfect pizza for your fiesta night. Load this pizza up with any of your favourite vegetables. Guacamole is totally, 100% optional but recommended. And margaritas, but you didn't hear that from me.

1. Prepare the dough by mixing 1 cup of the flour with the rest of the dry ingredients in a large bowl. Add the water and mix until a sticky dough forms, then gradually add the remaining flour. Add more flour if necessary. Once a dough ball has formed, transfer to a floured surface and gently knead for 3–4 minutes until smooth and elastic. Place the dough ball in an oiled bowl, cover with a tea towel and let rest for 10 minutes.

2. While the dough rests, prepare your toppings. For the sweet chilli sauce, simply whisk the ingredients together in a bowl and set aside.

3. To create your Tex-Mex bean mix, lightly fry the onion and garlic in coconut oil over a medium-high heat until fragrant. Add the black beans, corn, stock powder, coconut sugar, spices and salt and pepper and fry for a further 3–4 minutes. Remove from the heat and set aside.

4. Preheat your oven to 190°C/375°F and begin to roll out your dough until it is approximately 1cm thick. (Or roll it thinner if you'd like a thinner base.)

5. Spread the sweet chilli sauce evenly around the base, leaving a 2cm gap around the edges to create the crust. Top with vegan cheese, Tex Mex bean mix, sliced yellow (bell) pepper and sliced cherry tomatoes.

6. Bake the pizza in the preheated oven for 15–20 minutes until crispy around the edges.

7. Let the pizza sit for a few minutes prior to serving. Drizzle with some Vegan Sour Cream and garnish with coriander leaves.

TANDOORI CHICKPEA PIZZA
WITH COCONUT MINT YOGURT

MAKES
1
LARGE PIZZA

For the tandoori chickpeas:
1 × 400g (14oz) can chickpeas,
    rinsed and drained
175ml (⅔ cup) coconut cream
1 teaspoon harissa paste
1 tablespoon lemon juice
2 teaspoons ground cumin
1 teaspoon ground allspice
½ teaspoon ground cinnamon
1 teaspoon ground ginger
1 teaspoon smoked paprika
1 teaspoon garlic powder
1 teaspoon onion powder
½ teaspoon black pepper
½ teaspoon salt
2 teaspoons coconut sugar

For the easy pizza dough:
240g (2 cups) plain
    (all-purpose) flour
½ teaspoon salt
1 teaspoon ground turmeric
1 tablespoon raw cane sugar
1 tablespoon instant
    dry yeast*
200ml (⅔ cup plus
    2 tablespoons) of
    luke-warm water

**For the coconut and
mint yogurt:**
120g (1 cup) raw cashews,
    soaked for 3–6 hours
170ml (⅔ cup) coconut cream
1 tablespoon maple syrup
    or agave nectar

Tandoori chicken was one of my favourite Indian foods to order while growing up, paired with that magical mint yogurt they used to serve – I'm drooling thinking about it. But hey, you know what – how about we turn that into a pizza? (Yes, this is how my brain works.) Well, let's just say it was a very, very good idea. Here you go!

1. Prepare the tandoori chickpeas the night before (or at least 3–4 hours before) by mixing all of the ingredients in a small bowl. Cover and refrigerate.

2. Prepare the coconut and mint yogurt by blending all of the ingredients in a high-speed blender until no lumps remain. Store in an airtight container in the refrigerator until ready to use. (Any leftovers can be kept for up to a week and work wonderfully as a dip or salad dressing!)

3. Prepare the dough by mixing half of the flour with the rest of the dry ingredients in a large bowl. Add the water and mix until a sticky dough forms, then gradually add the remaining flour. Add more water or flour if necessary. Once a dough ball has formed, transfer to a floured surface and gently knead for 3–4 minutes until smooth and elastic. Place the dough ball in an oiled bowl, cover with a tea towel and let rest for 10 minutes. After 10 minutes, roll the pizza into a circle measuring 30cm/12 inches across. When ready to bake your pizza, preheat your oven to 190°C/375°F.

4. Place the pizza base on a large, lined baking tray and begin to top it by arranging your desired amount of vegan cheese first, followed by the tandoori chickpeas and finely sliced carrot, red (bell) pepper and onion.

2 tablespoons lemon juice

2 tablespoons apple
    cider vinegar

2 handfuls mint leaves

1 handful coriander leaves

1 tablespoon sunflower
    or olive oil

salt and pepper, to taste

For the toppings:

grated vegan cheese of choice

very thinly sliced purple
    carrot (or regular carrot)

finely diced red (bell) pepper
    and white onion

5. Bake in the preheated oven for 15–20 minutes, or until the edges are golden and crispy.

6. Allow to sit for 5 minutes before slicing. Finish with a drizzle (or desired amount) of coconut mint yogurt and enjoy.

* Ensure you are using INSTANT dry yeast not active yeast. This recipe requires no proofing (or proving, depending on where you are from).

CLASSIC PEPPERONI PIZZA

MAKES
«··· 1 ···»
LARGE PIZZA

For the spicy walnut meat:
100g (1 cup) activated
    walnuts, crushed
1 tablespoon soy sauce
1 tablespoon olive oil
½ teaspoon ground cumin
½ teaspoon chilli powder
½ teaspoon paprika
½ teaspoon onion powder

For the pizza dough:
240g (2 cups) plain
    (all-purpose) flour
½ teaspoon salt
½ teaspoon cumin
1 tablespoon raw sugar
1 tablespoon instant dry yeast
170ml (⅔ cup) plus 2 tablespoons
    luke-warm water

For the tomato sauce:
250ml (1 cup) salt-reduced
    tomato purée (paste)
6 sundried tomatoes
1 garlic clove
2 teaspoons coconut sugar
½ teaspoon salt

For the vegan pepperoni:
2 × vegan sausages
    (store-bought, or use
    my recipe page 118)
¼ teaspoon chilli powder
½ teaspoon smoked paprika
¼ teaspoon onion powder
1 tablespoon olive oil

For the toppings:
90–135g (1–1½ cups)
    grated vegan cheese
    (brand of choice)

A vegan twist on a traditional classic! Friday night was always take-out night when I was younger, and I remember one of my favourite pizza flavours was 'Meat Lovers' (what a great name, huh?) Now... seeing as I don't love meat anymore, I had to think of a way to recreate that favourite of mine, and then this beautiful thing was born. The dough recipe here is a super simple one!

1. Prepare the spicy walnut 'meat' a few hours beforehand by mixing the crushed walnuts with the soy sauce, oil, spices and onion powder. Set aside to marinate for at least 3 hours.

2. Prepare the dough by mixing half of the flour with the rest of the dry ingredients in a large bowl. Add the water and mix until a sticky dough forms, then gradually add the remaining flour. Add more flour or liquid if needed. Once a dough ball has formed, transfer to a floured surface and gently knead for 3–4 minutes until smooth and elastic. Place the dough ball in an oiled bowl, cover with a tea towel and let rest for 10 minutes.

3. To prepare the tomato sauce, simply blend the ingredients in a high-speed blender until smooth. Set aside.

4. Slice the sausages into thin slices. Fry over a medium-high heat in the coconut oil and spices until crispy. Be careful not to overcook as they will continue to cook in the oven.

5. Preheat your oven to 190°C/375°F. Roll your dough into a circle measuring 30cm/12 inches across and place on a lined baking tray.

6. Top your pizza with an even spread of the tomato sauce (leave a gap for the crust), a generous serving of vegan cheese, walnut 'meat' and the 'pepperoni'.

7. Bake in the preheated oven for 15–20 minutes until golden.

SATAY TOFU & NOODLES

SERVES
《··· 2 ···》

For the satay sauce:
100g (½ cup) organic
    peanut butter
125ml (½ cup) coconut milk
60ml (¼ cup) low-sodium
    vegetable stock, plus
    more if needed
3–4 tablespoons tamari
2 garlic cloves
3-cm/1-inch piece of ginger
1 teaspoon treacle or
    blackstrap molasses
1½ tablespoons maple syrup
2 teaspoons onion powder
juice of ½ lemon
salt, to taste
few drops of toasted
    sesame oil

For the tofu:
250g (2 cups) firm tofu
    (drained from any
    liquid and cut into
    bite-sized cubes)
1 tablespoon peanut oil
any thinly sliced vegetables
    of choice (broccoli, red
    peppers, mushrooms etc.)

To serve:
noodles of choice (pictured
    are black bean noodles)
sesame seeds
coriander leaves

This recipe is super easy and you'll have it on the table in no time. Serve this over your favourite noodles.

Feel free to substitute the tofu for any beans or vegetables of your choice.

1. Prepare the satay sauce by blending the ingredients in a high-speed blender until smooth. Add extra water if necessary to reach your desired consistency. Set aside.

2. Cook your noodles of choice by following the packet instructions. Rinse and drain and set aside.

3. In a non-stick frying pan, fry the tofu in the oil for a few minutes on each side until crispy. Add any vegetables you desire at this stage as well. Fry until the vegetables are tender.

4. Add the satay sauce to the pan and stir until the tofu is well coated. Simmer for 3–4 minutes until hot and the sauce has coated everything. Season to taste.

5. Serve the satay tofu over the noodles. Garnish with sesame seeds and a few coriander leaves.

VEGAN PHO

SERVES
≪··· 2 ···≫

For the broth:
1 brown onion, peeled
    and quartered
2 garlic cloves, minced
1 tablespoon coconut oil
1 litre (4 cups) vegetable stock
3-cm (1-inch) piece of ginger,
    thinly sliced into coins
2 cinnamon sticks
3 whole cloves
3 star anise
3 tablespoons soy sauce

To serve:
200g (2 cups) rice noodles
150g (1¼ cups) firm tofu, cut
    into 1cm (⅜ inch) cubes
1 tablespoon peanut oil
enoki mushrooms
pak choy (bok choy),
    stems removed
spring onion (green onion),
    sliced
fresh coriander leaves
1 teaspoon toasted sesame oil

I used to think I was funny and throw around "pho" puns until I learned it's pronounced "fuh" – so, hey – you learn something everyday. Anyway, this is a quick, simplified version of traditional pho, yet it's still really flavourful and delicious.

1. Place the onion and garlic in a large, deep saucepan and fry in the coconut oil over a medium-high heat until slightly browned.

2. Add the rest of the broth ingredients to the pan. Bring to the boil, then reduce to a simmer and cover for 30–40 minutes.

3. Cook the rice noodles by following the packet insrtuctions.

4. Lightly fry the tofu cubes in the peanut oil until golden and crispy. Add the enoki mushrooms and pak choi (bok choy) to the pan and fry for a further 1–2 minutes. Remove from the heat.

5. Take the broth off the heat and let it sit for a few minutes. Strain out any large chunks of spices and onions.

6. Prepare your pho by serving the cooked rice noodles in a serving bowl, followed by some hot broth, tofu, a few enoki mushrooms, a few pak choi (bok choy) leaves, sliced spring onion (green onion), fresh coriander leaves and a little sesame oil.

ROAST VEGGIE TACOS

MAKES
《⋯ 8–10 ⋯》
TACOS

1 large sweet potato, peeled
1 large potato, peeled
1 parsnip, peeled
1 tablespoon melted
    coconut oil
3 teaspoons coconut nectar
    or maple syrup
1 teaspoon vegetable bouillon
1 teaspoon ground cumin
1 teaspoon onion powder
salt and pepper, to taste

For the maple Dijon sauce:
2 teaspoons Dijon mustard
2 heaped teaspoons tahini
2 tablespoons maple syrup
¼ teaspoon salt
hot water, to thin

To serve:
8–10 corn tortillas
chard leaves
diced avocado
Aoili (page 196, optional)
black sesame seeds
lime or lemon

These tacos are a little different than the norm. However, I love the sweet and savoury combinations of the roast vegetables and the tang of the awesome Dijon sauce. Give it a whirl! It's great for a light breakfast, lunch or dinner to share with friends.

1. Preheat your oven to 190°C/375°F.

2. Cut the potatoes and parsnip into small cubes. In a large mixing bowl, coat the vegetables in coconut oil, coconut nectar or maple syrup, bouillon, cumin and onion powder and season with salt and pepper. Transfer to a lined roasting pan and bake in the oven for 55–60 minutes until golden, tossing half way. (Keep an eye on them as oven times will vary.)

3. In the meantime, whisk together the maple Dijon sauce ingredients and set aside.

4. Once the vegetables are done, it's time to start assembling! Simply warm the corn tortillas in a hot pan or microwave.

5. To assemble, start with a few chard leaves, a good handful of the roast vegetables, some diced avocado, a drizzle of maple Dijon sauce and aioli.

6. Finish with black sesame seeds and a squeeze of lime or lemon.

VEGAN SAUSAGES

MAKES
《··· **8–10** ···》
APPROXIMATELY

150g (1¼ cups) firm
tofu, cubed
1 × 400g red kidney beans,
rinsed and drained
1 teaspoon ground mustard
2 garlic cloves, minced
2 tablespoons soy sauce
1 tablespoon vegetable oil
125ml (½ cup) water
1 teaspoon coconut sugar
2 teaspoons liquid smoke
or smoked paprika
1–2 teaspoons vegetable
bouillon
2 teaspoons onion powder
½ teaspoon ground sage
½ teaspoon nutmeg
1 teaspoon ground cumin
¼ teaspoon ground
black pepper
156g (1¼ cups) vital wheat
gluten flour
2 tablespoons chickpea flour
(gram flour)
coconut oil, for frying

Equipment:
large pot, steamer basket
and lid or bamboo steamer
10 sheets of baking paper
10 sheets of aluminium
foil (approximately
10–15 × 20–30cm for
each sheet)

A delicious plant-based sausage – perfect for your Sunday breakfast, hot dogs or sliced on pizza! Steaming the seitan gives it a firm yet tender texture, so either a traditional steaming method or a bamboo steamer will do the trick.

1. Begin by blending the water, oil, tofu, kidney beans, garlic, coconut sugar, mustard, liquid smoke, soy sauce, bouillon, onion powder, sage and spices in a food processor or a high-speed blender until a smooth purée forms.

2. In a large bowl, whisk together the gluten flour and chickpea flour.

3. Make a well in the dry ingredients and pour in the bean purée. Mix with a rubber spatula and ensure you scrape down the sides of the bowl. Begin mixing with your hands until all of the flour has combined with the wet ingredients. The mixture will begin to form a soft dough ball – be careful not to overmix it.

4. Tear the dough into 8–10 even sections. Roll these sections out into sausage shapes (Make them slightly shorter than your pieces of baking paper and so you can twist the ends, around 10cm long)

5. Lay the baking paper on top of the foil and then place the sausage in the centre of the baking paper. Neatly roll it up (as if you are rolling sushi) in both the foil and paper so it is secure – if it is not secure enough the sausages will burst out during steaming. Twist the foil at both ends and ensure these are very secure as well.

6. Fill a large pot with water to just under the steamer basket and bring it to the boil. Arrange your sausages in the steamer basket (it is okay if they are touching) and cover.

7. Steam for 30 minutes. Uncover and let the sausages cool in the basket, then transfer them to the refrigerator to chill overnight (this will help them set further). Keep them wrapped in the baking paper and foil and unwrap as needed. They will keep in the refrigerator for up for 5 days.

8. When ready to use, unwrap the hot dogs and pan-fry or grill in oil for a few minutes on each side until golden and slightly crispy.

SEITAN CUTLETS

MAKES
5–6
APPROXIMATELY

190g (1½ cups) gluten flour
1 teaspoon onion powder
½ teaspoon garlic powder
1 tablespoon nutritional yeast
½ teaspoon ground cumin
½ teaspoon dried sage
1 tablespoon 'chicken'
    stock powder (check the
    ingredients to ensure
    it is vegan)
250ml (1 cup) water
1 tablespoon soy sauce
1 teaspoon olive oil
250ml (1 cup) vegetable
    stock, for baking (you
    may need more or less
    depending on the size
    of your baking dish)

Use these cutlets in place of chicken, beef or pork in any recipe!

1. Preheat the oven to 180°C/350°F.

2. Mix together the gluten flour, onion powder, garlic powder, yeast, cumin and sage in a large mixing bowl.

3. Whisk together the stock powder, water, soy sauce and olive oil.

4. Make a well in the gluten flour and pour in the wet ingredients, scraping down the sides of the bowl as you go. The gluten flour will begin to form a dough ball.

5. Transfer to a clean work surface and knead the dough for a few minutes to develop the gluten. It will begin to feel stretchy.

6. Allow the dough to sit for 5 minutes, then knead gently once more.

7. Cut the dough into 5–6 small sections or 'cutlets'. Stretch the cutlets with your hands until they are around 2–2.5cm thick.

8. Lay the cutlets in a 20×20 cm (8×8 inch) baking dish and add the vegetable stock (do not submerge them – you only want the stock to come 1 cm up the cutlets) and bake for 45–50 minutes uncovered, turning them over halfway. Bake until the cutlets have started to brown and form a slightly firm exterior.

9. Remove the cutlets from the broth and drain on a paper towel for a few minutes. Once cooled slightly, transfer to a resealable plastic bag and chill for 1–2 hours. (They will keep in the refrigerator for up to 5 days.) To use the cutlets, simply slice into pieces and grill or fry in oil until crispy and browned, or bread and deep fry using my recipe on page 58 (pictured on next page).

CHAPTER
···· 3 ····

SANDWICHES
&
BURGERS

BIG VEGAN BURGER

MAKES
≪··· 4 ···≫

For the burger patties:
180g (2 cups) TVP soy mince
    (dry measure)
1 red onion, finely chopped
1 tablespoon vegetable oil
1 × 400g can black beans,
    rinsed and drained
2–3 tablespoons plain
    (all-purpose) flour
2 tablespoons cornflour
1 heaped tablespoon ground
    flaxseeds
1 tablespoon maple syrup
2 teaspoons vegetable bouillon
    or paste (page 200)
2 teaspoons liquid smoke
    (hickory or mesquite)
1 tablespoon soy sauce
2 teaspoons garlic powder
2 teaspoons onion powder
1 teaspoon smoked paprika
½ teaspoon nutmeg
salt and pepper, to taste

**For the 'Big Mac'
mayonnaise:**
80ml (⅓ cup) vegan
    mayonnaise
1 tablespoon Dijon mustard
½ tablespoon ketchup
1 teaspoon onion powder
1 tablespoon maple syrup
½ teaspoon vegetable bouillon
    or paste (page 200)

There was something about Big Macs that really pulled my heart strings. Maybe it was the processed beef. Maybe it was the processed cheese. Or maybe, it was that sauce. That elusive, Big Mac sauce that just made your mouth explode.

Well, seeing as I'm now vegan, I can't (and don't want to) enjoy any of that. But I wanted to challenge myself to recreate that childhood flavour and memory, and the result this is beyond delicious!

· ·

1. Prepare your patties first by soaking the TVP in warm water by following the packet instructions and setting aside so it expands and absorbs all of the water. Preheat your oven to 180°C/350°F.

2. Lightly fry the red onion over a medium heat in the oil until it is fragrant and slightly caramelised.

3. In a food processor or high-speed blender, process the black beans and fried onion to a thick paste.

4. Combine the TVP, black bean purée, flour, cornflour, ground flaxseeds, syrup, stock, liquid smoke, soy sauce, garlic and onion powders and spices in a large bowl until a soft, sticky dough forms. It should be firm enough to shape into patties. Cover the bowl with some clingfilm and chill for 10 minutes. After 10 minutes, shape the mixture into your desired patty sizes or shapes.

5. Heat some more vegetable oil in a non-stick frying pan and fry each burger patty for 3–4 minutes on each side until the outside is nice and crispy. I like to cover the pan on the second flip to help it cook through a little faster.

For the burger assembly:
vegan cheese slices
seeded burger buns
   (sliced in half)
shredded iceberg lettuce
sliced pickles

6. Transfer them to a lined baking tray and place a slice of vegan cheese on top of each patty – keep them in the warm in the oven while you prepare your sauces and burger fillings so the cheese can melt slightly.

7. Prepare the 'Big Mac' mayonnaise by whisking all the ingredients together in a small bowl with a fork. Set aside.

8. Warm the buns in the oven or under the grill.

9. It's time to assemble your burgers! You can either stack these one or two patties high, but for presentation purposes I chose to go two patties high to achieve that authentic 'Big Mac' look. To assemble, spread a thin layer of Big Mac sauce on the bottom of a bun, followed by shredded lettuce, a cheese-topped patty and some sliced pickles. If you are double stacking, repeat the same procedure for the second layer.

10. Serve with oven-baked fries of your choice and ketchup. For simple homemade fries see my Chilli 'Cheese' Fries (page 166) and simply skip the cheese sauce and chilli sauce additions.

. . . .

HANDY TIPS:
··• If you are in a rush, keep an eye out at your local grocer for organic frozen fries (pictured) – these generally have less seasoning and oil in them. Simply follow the packet instructions but don't use oil, they don't need it and they will be delicious and crispy without it. Obviously this doesn't have to be your first option, but it's a great substitution. I'm all about balance!

BEET AND BLACK BEAN BURGER

MAKES

《··· 4 ···》

For the patties:
70g (¾ cup) wholegrain oats
130g (1 cup) raw almonds
1 beetroot (210–230g)
1 × 400g (14oz) can black
    beans, rinsed and drained
1–2 tablespoons olive oil
50g (½ cup) ground flaxseed
2 teaspoons dried parsley
2 teaspoons onion powder
2 teaspoons ground cumin
2 teaspoons ground cardamom
2 teaspoons vegetable bouillon
    or paste (page 200)
½ teaspoon black pepper
coconut oil, for frying

For the burger assembly:
2 sourdough buns
4 tablespoons Walnut & Kale
    Pesto (page 190)
1 large, ripe avocado
greens of choice
Tahini Coconut & Lime Mayo
    (page 180) or Maple Tahini
    Mayo (page 189)

With these beetroot patties, it's almost as if you are eating pink falafel, and I'm totally okay with that. The sweet beetroot pairs well with the mayo, kale pesto and leafy greens. I never used to like beetroot, but it's becoming one of my favourite vegetables to cook and bake with. For any vegetable haters out there – give them this! They'll never realise it's actually good for you.

1. You'll want to make the patty mixture a few hours before or ideally the night before. Begin by simply blending the oats and almonds in a high-speed blender or food processor until a fine meal forms. Set aside in a bowl.

2. Chop the beetroot into small chunks (you do not need to precook the beetroot) and blend it with the black beans in a high-speed blender until it forms a thick purée.

3. Combine the oat and almond mixture, purée, olive oil and other patty ingredients (except the coconut oil) in a bowl until well combined. Cover and leave in the refrigerator for a few hours or overnight – this will allow the mixture to set and ensures you have delicious, round patties!

4. When ready to prepare your burgers, preheat your oven to 160–170°C (325–350°F).

5. Shape your mixture into four patties and heat up some coconut oil in a large frying pan. Fry each patty for 2–3 minutes on each side until crispy.

6. Transfer the patties to a lined baking tray and place in the preheated oven. This will ensure they cook further while you prepare the rest of the burger components.

7. Slice the sourdough buns and warm in the oven or under the grill. Slice the avocado and wash any greens of your choice.

8. To assemble the burgers, simply spread a thick layer of pesto on the base bun. Layer the patty, avocado, greens and mayo of choice.

CASHEW & SWEET POTATO BURGERS

MAKES
《···· 4 ····》

For the patties:
120g (1 cup) raw cashew nuts
200g (2 cups) cooked and
    mashed sweet potato
2 carrots
50g (½ cup) ground flaxseeds
2 teaspoons onion powder
2 teaspoons ground cumin
1 teaspoon ground nutmeg
½ teaspoon cayenne pepper
½ teaspoon turmeric
½ teaspoon cinnamon
2 teaspoons vegetable bouillon
    or paste (page 200)
1 tablespoon coconut sugar
2–3 tablespoons plain
    (all purpose) flour
2 tablespoons coconut oil,
    for frying

**For the tomato and
harissa sauce:**
1 tablespoon salt-reduced
    tomato purée (paste)
1 teaspoon harissa paste
1 tablespoon maple syrup
1 teaspoon onion powder
salt, to taste

**For the creamy avocado
coconut dressing:**
½ large ripe avocado
60ml (¼ cup) coconut milk
juice of 1 lemon
small handful of mint leaves
salt, to taste

Sweet potatoes are hands-down (at the moment) one of my favourite foods, so I wanted to create a pretty epic burger out of 'em! This recipe can easily be made gluten-free by choosing a gluten-free flour and bun.

1. Prepare the patties a few hours ahead or the night before. Begin by pulsing the cashew nuts into a fine meal using a high-speed blender or food processor. Set aside in a bowl.

2. Chop the carrots and then blend the sweet potato and carrots into a thick purée. Set aside in a large bowl.

3. Mix the cashew meal, purée and the remaining patty ingredients together until it forms a dough. Add more flour if needed. Cover the bowl and allow the mixture to cool for a few hours, or overnight. This will ensure you have beautiful patties!

4. When you are ready to make your burgers, preheat your oven to 160–170°C (325–350°F).

5. Heat up some coconut oil in a large frying pan and fry two patties at a time for 2–3 minutes on each side until crispy. Transfer the patties to the preheated oven and place them on a baking tray lined with baking paper. Keep them in the oven while you make the rest of the components – the heat of the oven will continue to cook them and keep them warm.

6. Prepare the tomato and harissa sauce by whisking all the ingredients in a bowl. Set aside.

7. Prepare the creamy avocado dressing by blending the ingredients in a high-speed blender until thick and creamy. Set aside in a small bowl and refrigerate until ready to use.

For the burgers:
4 wholegrain buns
1 large tomato, sliced
greens of choice

8. Slice the buns and warm in the oven or under the grill.

9. To assemble your burger, spread the base of the bun with some tomato and harissa sauce. Top with a patty, followed by some slices of tomato, fresh greens and then a generous dollop of the avocado dressing.

10. Top with the final bun and serve.

MUSHROOM & 'BACON' BURGER

MAKES
«··· 2 ···»

1–2 portobello mushrooms
(depending on size)
1 tablespoon coconut oil
2 buns of choice
2 handfuls of mixed shredded
kale, carrot and red cabbage
salt and pepper, to taste

For the tempeh 'bacon':
4 thin strips tempeh
2 tablespoons tamari
1 teaspoon liquid smoke
1 tablespoon maple syrup
½ teaspoon onion powder
½ teaspoon garlic powder
1 teaspoon smoked paprika
1 teaspoon oil, for frying

For the quick garlic mayo:
3 tablespoons vegan
mayonnaise
1 teaspoon garlic powder
1 teaspoon onion powder
salt, to taste

Before going vegan, mushroom and bacon was one of my favourite food combinations. This plant-based version of sliders is super easy and super tasty. I like using tempeh bacon but it's also really great with my Super Rad Coconut Bacon (page 200).

1. Prepare the tempeh 'bacon' by marinating the strips of tempeh in the tamari, liquid smoke, maple syrup, onion powder, garlic powder and paprika for 30 minutes.

2. Prepare the mayonnaise by whisking the vegan mayonnaise with the garlic and onion powder. Season to taste and set this aside until you are ready to assemble.

3. Just before the tempeh has finished marinating, remove the stem from the portobello mushroom(s) and heat the coconut oil in a frying pan. Lightly fry the mushroom(s) for 1–2 minutes on each side, covering the pan with a lid when cooking the second side to allow it to cook through. Remove from the heat and drain on a paper towel.

4. Fry your tempeh strips in oil in the same pan as the mushroom for 3–4 minutes on each side until crispy.

5. To assemble your burger, simply spread a little mayo on the base of a bun followed by some shredded vegetables, then layer with the tempeh bacon and either half a portobello mushroom or a whole one, depending on the size.

6. Season with salt and pepper to taste and finish off with a little more mayonnaise.

'BLT' WITH AVOCADO

MAKES
⟪⋯ 2 ⋯⟫

2 buns of choice
 (or 4 slices bread)
1 ripe avocado, sliced
cos or iceberg lettuce
1 large tomato, sliced
3 tablespoons vegan
 mayonnaise
salt and pepper, to taste

For the tempeh 'bacon':
4 thin strips tempeh
2 tablespoons tamari
1 teaspoon liquid smoke
1 tablespoon maple syrup
½ teaspoon onion powder
½ teaspoon garlic powder
1 teaspoon smoked paprika
1 teaspoon oil, for frying

A true classic! This is super easy and I've given you the option of either tempeh bacon or my Super Rad Coconut Bacon (page 200), so definitely try both and see which you prefer.

• •

1. Prepare the tempeh bacon by marinating the strips of tempeh in the tamari, liquid smoke, maple syrup, onion powder, garlic powder and paprika for at least 30–60 minutes.

2. Once the tempeh has marinated for 30–60 minutes, heat a little oil in a frying pan and fry the strips for 3–4 minutes on each side, covering the pan with a lid when cooking the second side. Pour the remaining marinade over the tempeh on the second side. It should be slightly browned and smokey around the edge once finished.

3. To assemble your 'BLT', slice the bun in half and layer it with avocado, lettuce, the tempeh bacon, tomato and a generous serving of vegan mayonnaise. Season to taste.

SATAY TOFU SANDWICH STACK

MAKES
《⋯ 1 ⋯》

2 thin strips firm tofu
    (approximately 0.5cm
    (¼ inch) thick)
a few slices of red onion
1 tablespoon coconut oil
2 slices bread of choice
½ ripe avocado, mashed
1 small tomato, sliced
a small handful of alfalfa
    sprouts

For the quick satay sauce:
2 tablespoons peanut butter
1 tablespoon boiling water
½ tablespoon tamari
1 tablespoon maple syrup
1 teaspoon onion powder
salt, to taste

A delicious and easy sandwich idea for a lunch-in-a-rush, whether at school or at work!

1. Begin by lightly frying the tofu and red onion slices in a large frying pan in the coconut oil until the tofu is crispy on both sides and the onion is soft.

2. Prepare the satay sauce by whisking the ingredients together in a small bowl. Set aside.

3. Toast your bread, then assemble your sandwich.

4. Using a fork, spread a thick layer of avocado on one slice of bread. Layer it with tomato, onion, alfalfa sprouts and the slices of tofu. Spread the satay sauce on the last piece of bread and place on top. Enjoy!

BBQ PULLED 'PORK' SLIDERS
WITH COLESLAW

SERVES
≪⋯ 2 ⋯≫

1 × 560g (20oz) can young
  green jackfruit in brine
  or water
1 brown onion, chopped
1 garlic clove, minced
1 tablespoon peanut oil
3 tablespoons BBQ sauce
1–2 teaspoons liquid smoke
1 teaspoon blackstrap
  molasses or black treacle
1½ teaspoons onion powder
½ teaspoon ground nutmeg
2 teaspoons smoked paprika
125ml (½ cup) vegetable stock
salt and pepper, to taste

For the cashew mayo:
120g (1 cup) cashews,
  soaked for 3–6 hours
175ml (⅔ cup) soy milk
60ml (¼ cup) olive oil
1 tablespoon maple syrup
  or coconut nectar
1 teaspoon onion powder
1 tablespoon apple cider
  vinegar
salt, to taste
water, if needed

To serve:
2 cups shredded carrots,
  cabbage and onion
3–4 buns of choice
fried onions (optional)

Jackfruit is seriously a game changer when it comes to creating vegan 'meat'. You can usually find it at Asian grocery stores or online, but ensure you get the young green jackfruit in water or brine, not the syrupy one! Impress your friends and family with these smokey BBQ 'Pork' Sliders.

1. Prepare the cashew mayo by blending the ingredients in a high-speed blender for a few minutes until no lumps remain.

2. Mix together the shredded carrots, cabbage and onions and the cashew mayo in a small bowl until well coated. Set the coleslaw mix aside in the refrigerator.

3. Drain and rinse the jackfruit. Slice or pull off the hard 'core' centre of the chunks of jackfruit, leaving the sinewy edges.

4. In a large frying pan, fry the onion and garlic in the peanut oil until fragrant. Add the jackfruit, BBQ sauce, liquid smoke, molasses, onion powder, spices and a few tablespoons of the vegetable stock to prevent it sticking to the pan.

5. Simmer this over a medium-high heat, and using a fork, begin to gently 'pull' the jackfruit until it shreds.

6. Slowly add the rest of the vegetable stock and keep stirring. Don't pull the jackfruit TOO much as it could become a little sloppy. You still want it slightly chunky.

7. Cover with a lid and simmer on a low heat for 3 minutes. Remove from the heat.

8. Warm the buns up in a pan, oven or microwave. To assemble, slice a bun in half and layer the base with the coleslaw mix. Spoon the 'pulled jackfruit' on top and finish with fried onions (this is optional) and the top of the bun.

CHILLI CHICKPEA SANDWICH

MAKES
《··· 2 ···》

1 × 400g (14oz) can chickpeas,
   rinsed and drained
2 tablespoons reduced-salt
   tomato purée (paste)
2 teaspoons hot sauce
   or sweet chilli sauce
   (plus more if you like)
1 tablespoon coconut nectar
   or maple syrup
1 teaspoon onion powder
1 teaspoon ground cumin
½ teaspoon dried thyme
salt and pepper, to taste
3–4 tablespoon of Cheesy
   Nacho Sauce (page 180)
4 thick slices sourdough or
   wholewheat bread, toasted
1 tablespoon vegan butter

One of my all-time favourites, and is incredibly popular over my social media platforms. Give it a whirl!

• •

1. Prepare the chickpeas by frying the chickpeas, tomato purée, hot sauce, coconut nectar, onion powder, cumin and thyme over a medium-high heat. Lightly press down on the chickpeas with a fork to break some of them up, but leave a few whole. Remove from the heat after a few minutes, season to taste, cover with a lid and set aside.

2. Heat the Cheesy Nacho Sauce in a small saucepan.

3. To assemble the sandwich, spread a layer of Cheesy Nacho Sauce on a piece of toast. Put a few tablespoons of the chickpea mixture on top and cover with the last piece of bread.

CHEESY BLACK BEAN NACHO BURGER
WITH SWEET CHILLI SAUCE

MAKES
2–3
BURGERS

For the patties:
1 tablespoon coconut oil
1 red onion, finely diced
1 × 400g (14oz) can of black
    beans, rinsed and drained
130g (1 cup) raw almonds
45g (½ cup) wholegrain oats
2 teaspoons garlic powder
2 teaspoons onion powder
1 teaspoon chipotle chilli powder
1 teaspoon smoked paprika
2 teaspoons ground cumin
2 teaspoons liquid smoke
    (or more paprika)
1–2 teaspoons vegetable
    bouillon or paste (page 200),
    to taste
80ml (⅓ cup) plant-based milk
2–3 tablespoons ground
    flaxseeds

For the sweet chilli sauce:
1–2 teaspoons hot sauce
    or chilli paste
2 tablespoons reduced-salt
    tomato purée/paste
2–3 tablespoons maple syrup
1 teaspoon garlic powder
1 teaspoon onion powder
½ teaspoon salt
water to thin, if necessary

To serve:
Cheesy Nacho Sauce (page 180)
1 vine tomato
1 ripe avocado
juice of ½ lime
salt and pepper, to taste
2–3 buns of choice
a few handfuls of corn chips
    (any vegan brand)

The name says it all! A lil' Tex-Mex twist to spice up your burger!

1. Prepare the patties at least 3 hours before making your burgers (or ideally overnight).

2. Heat the coconut oil in a frying pan and fry the red onion until it is slightly caramelised.

3. Blend the black beans and cooked onion in a high-speed blender or food processor until a thick paste forms. Set aside.

4. Blend the almonds and oats until they form a fine meal, then set aside in a large mixing bowl.

5. Add the garlic powder, onion powder, spices, black bean purée, liquid smoke, bouillon, milk and ground flax to the bowl and mix until well combined. For shape, I like to cover and refrigerate for 3 hours or overnight.

6. Preheat your oven to 150–160°C (300–325°F) when you are ready to make your burgers.

7. Shape the mixture into patties and fry over a medium heat in a little coconut oil for approximately 3–4 minutes on each side until crispy. Transfer them to a lined baking tray and keep them warm in the oven while you prepare the rest of the ingredients (they will continue to cook here, which is what you want).

8. Prepare the Cheesy Nacho Sauce by following the recipe (page 180) and prepare the sweet chilli sauce by whisking all the ingredients in a small bowl and set aside. Finely chop the tomato and set aside. Mash the avocado in a bowl with some lime juice and salt and pepper to taste. Set this aside also.

9. Warm the buns in the oven or under the grill.

10. To assemble your burger, spread some sweet chilli on the base of the burger bun followed by the patty, some Cheesy Nacho Sauce, crushed corn chips and chopped tomato. Spread some of the smashed avocado on the top of the bun and place on top.

SUSHI BURGER
WITH TERIYAKI TOFU STEAK

MAKES
≪··· 2–4 ···≫
BURGERS

For the sushi rice bun:
200g (1 cup) sushi rice
60ml (¼ cup) sushi vinegar

For the teriyaki tofu 'steak':
250g (2 cups) tofu, drained
3 tablespoons soy sauce
1 tablespoon mirin
2 tablespoons maple syrup
1 teaspoon garlic powder
1 teaspoon onion powder

For the cashew mayo:
120g (1 cup) cashews,
    soaked for 3–6 hours
175ml (⅔ cup) soy milk
60ml (¼ cup) olive oil
1 tablespoon maple syrup
    or coconut nectar
1 teaspoon onion powder
1 tablespoon apple cider
    vinegar
salt, to taste
water, if needed

For the fillings:
sliced avocado
pickled ginger
shredded purple cabbage
sesame seeds, for decoration

I shared this recipe on my social media platform a while back, and it received a lot of attention! This is also, might I add, simply just for fun! Eating sushi in burger form may not be the most practical of matters, but it's definitely fun for children and adults alike (I mean who doesn't like making rice buns, c'mon?!)

I recommend eating it with a knife and fork – as things can get a little messy.

1. To make the sushi rice bun, cook the sushi rice by following the packet instructions.

2. Mix the sushi vinegar through your cooked rice. Let the rice completely cool in the refrigerator before moulding.

3. Grab a small mug (mine was around 5cm (2 inches) in diameter) and quickly rinse it with water or grease with oil (this will stop the rice sticking), then press some rice into the bowl, filling it around three-quarters of the way up the bowl (this is for the top bun).

4. Turn it upside down and gently bang the bowl against a surface (like a wooden chopping board) to loosen the rice out out of the bowl. You now have your first top bun! Place it in the refrigerator and complete the same process using a little less rice for the bottom of the bun. Repeat the process again to make another bun.

5. To make the teriyaki tofu 'steak', cut the tofu into 2–4 large, thin squares so you have squares around 1 cm (3/8 inch) thick. Trim the edges with a knife to make a circular shape. (This is so the burger will fit together; you could simply just cut the tofu into thin strips but I will leave this to your personal preference!)

6. Whisk together the teriyaki ingredients and allow the tofu to sit in the marinade for 1 hour or overnight.

7. Fry the tofu in the marinade and a little oil in a frying pan for around 2–3 minutes on each side until crispy.

8. To make the cashew mayo, blend all the ingredients together for a couple of minutes in a high-speed blender or food processor, until everything is super smooth and creamy. Season to taste. Set aside in the refrigerator until ready to use. Keep any leftover cashew mayo in a sealed container in the refrigerator for 4–5 days.

9. To assemble your buns, place a thin layer of avocado on the bottom of one of your rice buns, followed by some cashew mayo, a slice of tofu, some pickled ginger and then shredded cabbage. VERY gently place the top bun on top.

10. Be gentle! They can be a little fiddly depending on how many fillings you choose to use, so please bear this in mind when assembling them. The burger is best eaten with cutlery. Enjoy!

• •

NOTE: These can also be made into bite-sized 'sliders' simply by using a smaller mould such as a mini cupcake mould to shape the buns.

'CHICKEN', CRANBERRY & CHEESE TOASTIE

MAKES
1
AWESOME SANDWICH

4–5 thin slices seitan
(store-bought or use
my recipe on page 120)
2 teaspoons coconut oil
1 × panini or bread roll
of choice
2 teaspoons vegan butter
40g (⅓ cup) grated vegan
cheese
2 teaspoons plant-based milk

For the cranberry jam:
60g (½ cup) dried cranberries,
soaked in hot water
overnight and drained
80ml (⅓ cup) maple syrup
1 teaspoon lemon juice
¼ teaspoon salt

When I was at high school I had a routine where every Friday I would order a chicken, cranberry and cheese panini from the school kitchen. Those things were my kryptonite. Well, turns out I don't really enjoy eating chicken and cheese that much anymore, unless it's vegan… and oh, wait – here's a vegan version! It's super good and an awesome treat for lunch or a light dinner, and it will please any meat eater in your family. In this 'toastie' I have pre-melted the cheese, as I've found that some vegan cheese brands don't melt how I'd like them to. This is totally optional, however.

1. Prepare the cranberry jam by blending the cranberries, maple syrup, lemon juice and salt in a high-speed blender or food processor for 60 seconds. Set aside and store in an airtight container.

2. Lightly fry the seitan in a pan with the coconut oil for 2–3 minutes until it is golden. Lay the slices on a paper towel to drain any excess oil.

3. Slice the panini in half and butter both sides. Grill the bread on a griddle pan or frying pan until golden.

4. To achieve 'stretchy' melted cheese, simply melt the vegan cheese in a small saucepan over a medium heat with 2 teaspoons of plant-based milk. Continuously stir until the cheese has completely melted. Consistency will vary depending on the brand of vegan cheese you are using, so adjust the liquid or add more cheese if you need too. Alternatively, feel free to melt your cheese under the grill.

5. To assemble, drizzle a thick layer of melted cheese on both slices of the panini. Layer the cranberry jam and seitan and sandwich together.

CHAPTER
···· 4 ····

SALADS
&
SIDES

RUSTIC POTATO SALAD
WITH COCONUT 'BACON'

SERVES
2
OR MORE AS A SIDE

For the salad:
6–7 medium–large roasting
    potatoes, peeled
1–2 tablespoons olive oil
60g (1 cup) finely shredded
    red cabbage
2 handfuls of chopped spring
    onion (green onion)
2 celery stalks, finely chopped
2 tablespoons finely chopped
    chives

For the dressing:
1 serving Creamy Vegan
    Mayonnaise (page 186)
2 tablespoons sweet
    pickle relish
1 teaspon Dijon mustard
2 teaspoons onion powder
2 teaspoons dill leaf tips
1 teaspoon dried parsley
salt and pepper, to taste

For the coconut bacon:
40g (½ cup) coconut flakes
3 tablespoons tamari
2 teaspoons liquid smoke
1 tablespoon maple syrup
1 teaspoon onion powder
1 teaspoon paprika
1 tablespoon coconut oil

I made this salad as a dish for a work staff party and kept it in the fridge at work. Later that day, however, I found a group of the staff members pulling away at the seal on the container and eating it. So, safe to say – it didn't really completely make it to the party, but it was a compliment in itself. It's seriously so, so good and easy to make. Perfect for BBQs, summer or anytime of the year really.

1. Preheat your oven to 200°C/400°F.

2. Prepare the coconut bacon by coating coconut flakes in the tamari, liquid smoke, maple syrup, onion powder and paprika, and set aside.

3. Chop your potatoes into cubes and place them on a baking tray. Toss them in the olive oil and bake for around 40–45 minutes until they are crispy on the outside and soft in the centre. Allow the potatoes to cool before using them.

4. To make the dressing simply whisk all the ingredients together in a large bowl.

5. Cook the coconut bacon by lightly frying the coconut mixture in the coconut oil for 2–3 minutes. Keep stirring until it begins to caramelise. Remove from the heat.

6. It's time to assemble your salad! Simply toss the potatoes, the shredded and chopped vegetables and the dressing together until well combined.

7. Serve immediately or keep in the fridge for up to 3 days until you are ready to eat. Top with coconut bacon prior to serving.

SUPER GREENS SLAW

SERVES
«···1–2···»

70–100g (2–3 cups) finely
   chopped and stemmed kale
1 tablespoon olive oil
1 teaspoon Himalayan sea salt
60–120g (1–2 cups) finely
   shredded red cabbage
2 carrots, peeled with a
   julienne peeler
2–3 handfuls chopped spring
   onion (green onion)
3–4 tablespoons chopped
   parsley
4–5 tablespoons seeds of
   choice (e.g. pumpkin,
   sunflower, sesame)

**For the maple and tahini
mayo:**
3–4 tablespoons tahini
3 tablespoons apple cider
   vinegar
juice of ½ lemon
80ml (⅓ cup) maple syrup
¼ teaspoon sal, or to taste
pinch of ground black pepper
hot water (to thin, if needed)

I have this nearly every night of the week (it's probably the
tahini dressing that is the culprit here) but this is SUCH an
awesome way to up your salad game and to use up any salad
vegetables that are lying around in your fridge. Shred and
finely slice everything, toss it together with the dressing
and you have one killer salad.

1. In a large bowl, mix the kale, olive oil and salt. Gently massage
the kale with your hands until it begins to break up and soften.
You don't want it soggy, so be careful not to over-work.

2. To prepare the maple and tahini mayo, simply whisk everything
in a bowl until you reach your desired consistency.

3. Gently toss the kale mixture and the remaining salad
ingredients together. Add the maple and tahini mayo and toss
together thoroughly.

4. Serve immediately or store covered in the refrigerator for
up to 2 days until you are ready to serve!

PESTO PASTA SALAD

SERVES
《··· 2 ···》

For the pasta salad:
200g (3 cups) pasta of choice
120g (1 cup) green peas
a handful of mint leaves,
    roughly chopped
1 lime
radish, sliced (optional)
black sesame seeds,
    to decorate

For the pesto:
2 garlic cloves
1 tablespoon coconut oil
60g (½ cup) walnuts
60g (½ cup) cashews
60g (1 cup) kale leaves,
    roughly chopped
30g (1 cup) basil leaves
125ml (½ cup) olive oil
60ml (¼ cup) water
½ teaspoon ground sea salt,
    or to taste
¼ teaspoon ground black
    pepper
½ teaspoon onion powder
2 teaspoons coconut sugar
1 tablespoon nutritional yeast

Pair your favourite pasta with my favourite pesto. This winning combination is rich in nutrients, refreshing and filling! I can never be bothered eating a giant salad, but I am also aware of how important it is to fill up on leafy greens – so what better way to meet these requirements by disguising it in... pasta.

1. Cook your pasta following the packet instructions.

2. To make the pesto, first lightly fry the garlic cloves in the coconut oil until they are fragrant. Blend all of the other pesto ingredients in a high-speed blender until smooth and creamy. Adjust the liquid if necessary. (Depending what pasta you use, you may want to add a little more water.)

3. Drain the pasta and rinse under cool water, transfer to a serving bowl and then stir through the pesto, peas and mint leaves.

4. Garnish with a squeeze of lime, sliced radish and sesame seeds. Serve immediately or keep stored and covered in the refrigerator for up to 3 days until ready to serve.

MOROCCAN CHICKPEA & SWEET POTATO SALAD

SERVES
≪··· 2 ···≫

For the salad:
4 small sweet potatoes
2–3 handfuls of shredded cabbage
2–3 handfuls of chopped spinach
20g (⅓ cup) finely chopped spring onion (green onion)

For the Moroccan chickpeas:
1 tablespoon coconut oil
1 garlic clove, minced
½ red onion, finely chopped
1 teaspoon cumin seeds
1 × 400g (14oz) can chickpeas, rinsed and drained
1 teaspoon paprika
½ teaspoon ground fennel
½ teaspoon ground nutmeg
½ teaspoon ground turmeric
2 tablespoons maple syrup
salt, to taste

To serve:
Maple Tahini Mayo (page 189)
flaked almonds
black sesame seeds

This is one of my staple salads and weeknight meals. It's super easy, fragrant and full of earthy flavours – which I love. Feel free to incorporate your favourite salad vegetables into the mix too!

1. Preheat your oven to 190°C/375°F and wrap your sweet potatoes in aluminium foil. Bake in the preheated oven for approximately 30–50 minutes (it may take longer depending on the size of your sweet potato) until they are cooked through.

2. To make the Moroccan chickpeas, first heat the coconut oil in a frying pan and sauté the garlic, onion and cumin seeds until the onion begins to brown. Add the chickpeas and remaining ingredients and lightly fry for around 2–3 minutes. Season with salt.

3. Assemble your cabbage, spinach and spring onion (green onion) on a plate in preparation for the sweet potatoes.

4. Remove your sweet potatoes from the oven and foil and lightly press down on them with a fork to 'smash' them into a slightly flatter shape.

5. Arrange them on top of the greens, and then top with your chickpeas.

6. Next, prepare the Maple Tahini Mayo and drizzle over the salad and potatoes.

7. Finish the salad with flaked almonds and black sesame seeds.

SPICY PEANUT & BROWN RICE SALAD

SERVES
2
OR MORE AS A SIDE

For the salad:
300g (2 cups) cooked brown
    rice, cooled
180–240g (3–4 cups) finely
    shredded red cabbage
3–4 carrots, grated or peeled
    using a julienne peeler
2–3 handfuls of mung-bean
    sprouts
1 × 300g (10½oz) can diced
    pineapple, drained of juice
2 handfuls of chopped spring
    onion (green onion)
1 handful of fresh coriander,
    chopped
1 teaspoon toasted sesame oil
60g (½ cup) raw peanuts,
    roughly chopped
1 ripe avocado, sliced
black sesame seeds, for
    decorating
lime, to serve

For the spicy peanut dressing:
3–4 tablespoons peanut butter
80ml (⅓ cup) coconut milk
80ml (⅓ cup) hot water
3 tablespoons tamari
1 teaspoon black treacle
    or blackstrap molasses
1½ tablespoons maple syrup
2 teaspoons onion powder
1 teaspoon garlic powder
2 teaspoons minced ginger
1 teaspoon harissa paste or
    ½ teaspoon chilli powder
juice of ½ lime or lemon
½ teaspoon sesame oil
salt, to taste

This salad is a great option for lunch or dinner. I make it regularly and love adding lots of variations of salad ingredients – depending on what I'm feeling like. The peanut sauce is one of my favourites – feel free to adjust the seasonings to suit your taste preferences! This salad stores well in the refrigerator and is a great way to use up leftover rice too!

1. Blend all of the dressing ingredients in a high-speed blender until smooth and set aside.

2. Toss the salad ingredients (everything apart from the peanuts, avocado and sesame seeds) until well combined.

3. Drizzle the dressing over the salad and gently toss together. (Use as much as you desire and save any leftover dressing in a sealed container in the refrigerator for up to 5 days)

4. Serve with the fresh avocado slices, black sesame seeds and a squeeze of lime.

CHICKPEA, APRICOT & ALMOND BROWN RICE SALAD

200g (1 cup) brown rice
1 × 400g (14oz) can chickpeas,
    rinsed and drained
1 tablespoon olive oil
1 tablespoon coconut sugar
2 teaspoons cumin seeds
1 teaspoon ground cardamom
1 teaspoon onion powder
1 teaspoon ground turmeric
65g (½ cup) chopped almonds
100–150g (approx. 3 cups)
    leafy greens, chopped
    (shard, kale or spinach)
spring onion (green onion),
    finely chopped
75g (½ cup) dried apricots,
    finely chopped
salt and pepper, to taste
squeeze of lemon or lime

For the almond coconut mayo:
65g (½ cup) blanched
    almonds, soaked in boiling
    water for 1 hour
125ml (½ cup) coconut milk
60ml (¼ cup) water
2 teaspoons apple cider
    vinegar
2 tablespoons maple syrup
1 tablespoon extra virgin
    olive oil
salt and pepper, to taste

A super refreshing, light and fragrant salad that the whole family will love.

1. Cook the brown rice following the packet instructions. Allow the rice to cool completely before using.

2. While the rice is cooling, preheat your oven to 200°C/400°F. After rinsing and draining the chickpeas, transfer them to a bowl and rub them with the olive oil, sugar, cumin seeds, cardamom, onion powder, turmeric and salt and pepper until well coated. Toss through the almonds. Transfer the mixture to a lined baking tray and bake in the oven until the chickpeas begin to 'pop' (around 15–20 minutes).

3. In a large salad bowl, combine the cooled brown rice, chopped leafy greens, onion and apricots and toss until well combined. Transfer the salad to a dish of choice, or simply keep it in the bowl you have just mixed it in. Remove the chickpeas from the oven and toss half of them through the salad, and decorate the top with the other half.

4. To prepare the almond coconut mayo, simply drain the almonds and blend all of the ingredients in a high-speed blender for 90 seconds until smooth. Thin with water if needed.

5. Drizzle the dressing over the salad and enjoy! Finish with a squeeze of lemon or lime.

CAESAR SALAD
WITH GARLIC CROUTONS AND ALMOND 'PARMESAN'

SERVES
«··· 2 ···»

For the croutons:
2–3 slices sourdough bread, cut
    into 2–3 cm (1 inch) cubes
1 tablespoon vegan butter, melted
1 teaspoon garlic powder
pinch of sea salt

For the Caesar dressing:
120g (1 cup) raw cashews,
    soaked for 3–6 hours
175ml (⅔ cup) soy milk
60ml (¼ cup) olive oil
1 teaspoon Dijon mustard
2 tablespoons lemon juice
1 teaspoon garlic powder
2 teaspoons onion powder
1 tablespoon nutritional yeast
½ tablespoon capers and brine
salt, to taste
water, if needed

For the coconut bacon:
2 teaspoons coconut oil
1 × 400g (14oz) can chickpeas,
    rinsed and drained
40g (½ cup) coconut flakes
1 teaspoon onion powder
1 teaspoon paprika
3 tablespoons tamari
2–3 teaspoons liquid smoke
1 tablespoons maple syrup

For the almond 'Parmesan':
65g (½ cup) almonds
30g (½ cup) nutritional yeast
1 teaspoon onion powder
1 teaspoon garlic powder
1 teaspoon sea salt

For the salad:
baby cos or butter lettuce
sliced spring onion (green onion)
sliced radish

A vegan take on one of my favourite salad combinations.
This is so delicious and perfect to take to BBQs, parties
or to eat all by yourself. Feel free to bulk it up and add
your favourite salad ingredients!

1. Preheat your oven to 200°C/400°F. Now, prepare your croutons
by tossing the bread, butter and garlic powder in a bowl until the
bread is coated evenly with butter. Transfer to a greased baking tray
and bake for 10–12 minutes until golden. Toss them over halfway.

2. While the croutons are baking, prepare the dressing by blending
the cashews, soy milk, oil, mustard, lemon juice and other ingredients
in a high-speed blender until thick and creamy. Add a little water
if you'd like a thinner sauce. Set aside in the fridge.

3. Prepare your almond 'Parmesan' by blitzing the almonds,
nutritional yeast, onion and garlic powders and salt in a high-speed
blender until a fine meal forms. Store in a sealed jar in the refrigerator
until ready to use. (This keeps well in the fridge for up to a week!)

4. Time for the crispy chickpea coconut 'bacon'. Simply heat
the coconut oil, chickpeas and coconut flakes in a frying pan over
a medium-high heat. Add the onion powder, paprika, tamari and
liquid smoke. Continue to stir, and when the chickpeas begin
to 'pop', add the maple syrup. Continue to fry until the coconut
begins to crisp but be careful not to burn it. Remove from the
heat immediately.

5. Build your salad by arranging a bed of cos lettuce, spring onion
and radish on a large plate.

6. Top with your 'bacon', a handful of croutons, a large drizzle of
dressing and some almond 'Parmesan'. Alternatively, please feel
free to finely chop your cos lettuce and mix everything in a large
mixing bowl until the dressing coats the salad well.

CHILLI 'CHEESE' FRIES

SERVES
≪⋯ 1–2 ⋯≫

4–6 large waxy potatoes,
    peeled
1–2 tablespoons melted
    coconut oil
salt and pepper, to taste
Cheesy Nacho Sauce
    (page 180)

For the sweet chilli sauce:
1–2 teaspoons hot sauce
    or chilli paste
2 tablespoons reduced-salt
    tomato purée/paste
2–3 tablespoons maple syrup
1 teaspoon garlic powder
1 teaspoon onion powder
½ teaspoon salt
water to thin, if necessary

**For the quick and easy
coconut bacon:**
see recipe on page 48

Basically an emotional hug on a plate. Except it's cruelty-free, and won't leave you feelin' crappy.

Serve with either the coconut 'bacon' recipe listed below or my Super Rad Coconut 'Bacon' on page 202.

1. Preheat the oven to 200°C/400°F.

2. Cut your potatoes into 1–2 cm (½–¾ inch) thick fries. In a large bowl, rub the potatoes in coconut oil until well coated. Transfer the chips to a baking tray (leaving around a 0.5cm (¼ inch) gap between each chip – this is the secret to crispy fries!) and bake for approximately 50 minutes, flipping them over halfway through until golden. The baking time WILL vary depending on your oven and how thinly you sliced the potatoes, so please be sure to keep an eye on them!

3. While the chips are cooking, prepare the sweet chilli sauce by whisking the ingredients together in a small bowl.

4. Prepare the coconut 'bacon'.

5. Prepare the Cheesy Nacho Sauce and simply heat this up just before you are about to serve your fries.

6. Once the fries are finished in the oven, season with a little salt and pepper and assemble on a plate or serving tray. Sprinkle with coconut bacon and drizzle both the hot nacho cheese and sweet chilli sauce over the top. (Use as much as you desire, and simply store any leftover sauce in a sealed container in the refrigerator for up to 5 days.)

ROOT VEGETABLE MASH

3 potatoes
2 large carrots
1 large sweet potato
½ brown onion
1 garlic clove
1 tablespoon coconut oil
1 tablespoon vegan butter
2 tablespoons nutritional
   yeast
2 tablespoons coconut sugar
1 teaspoon ground nutmeg
salt and pepper, to taste

If "Pimp My Mashed Potato" was a TV show, this would be the main star. This recipe is full of flavour, colour and is SO delicious either by itself or as a side. Give it a whirl!

1. Roughly chop and peel the potatoes, carrots and sweet potato. Bring to the boil in a large saucepan or steam until soft.

2. Finely dice the onion and garlic clove and fry with coconut oil in a frying pan until fragrant and caramelised. Set aside.

3. Once the root vegetables are cooked through, remove from the heat, drain the liquid and then place them back into the same pan.

4. Add the butter, nutritional yeast, coconut sugar and nutmeg to the root vegetables and roughly mash. Stir through the garlic and onion last. Season to taste.

SWEET 'N' SALTY POTATOES

SERVES
⟪⋯1–2⋯⟫

5–6 large roasting potatoes
2 tablespoons olive oil
3 tablespoons coconut sugar
1–2 teaspoons vegetable
    bouillon
3 teaspoons sweet paprika
2 teaspoons onion powder
1 teaspoon garlic powder
salt, to taste

It's sweet, it's salty... and it's so incredibly easy. These crispy morsels have been sent straight down from plant-based heaven for you to enjoy. I eat them by themselves, or paired with a side of creamy kale slaw. You can use any variety of potato you wish – my favourite is Dutch Cream! Feel free to add any herbs or spices you like.

1. Preheat your oven to 200°C/400°F.

2. Dice the potatoes into 2 cm (³⁄₄ inch) cubes. In a large mixing bowl, coat the potatoes well with olive oil, sugar, stock bouillon and spices. Transfer to a baking tray. Bake for 45–50 minutes until crispy, tossing over halfway.

3. Enjoy as a snack on their own or as a side.

ONION RINGS

SERVES
《··· *2–4* ···》

250ml (1 cup) soy milk
2 tablespoons apple
    cider vinegar
120g (1 cup) plain
    (all-purpose) flour
½ teaspoon garlic powder
1 teaspoon vegetable
    stock powder
2 brown onions, sliced
    into rings
2–3 tablespoons cornflour,
    for dusting
500–750ml (2–3 cups) oil
    (sunflower, peanut or
    vegetable), for frying
salt, for seasoning

For the aioli:
see recipe on page 189

Yeah, I know. This is a little naughty. But who doesn't love a good onion ring every now and then?!

These are definitely rings you can say "I do" to. Go ahead and make these to share with friends, or hide in your room and eat 'em. Up to you – but rest assured that these crispy morsels, paired with the creamy aioli, will bring a smile to your face.

1. Prepare the aioli first and store in the refrigerator while you prepare the onion rings.

2. Whisk together the soy milk mixture and apple cider vinegar. Set aside to thicken.

3. Whisk together the flour, garlic powder and stock powder.

4. Combine the soy milk into the dry ingredients and mix into a smooth and creamy thick batter. A few lumps are fine.

5. Heat the oil in a small saucepan to 180–190°C/350–375°F. (You want the oil to be at least 2–3 inches deep for deep-frying, so I find a smaller saucepan works better because you don't have to use as much oil.)

6. Working with one onion ring at a time, dust in cornflour then dip and coat the onion in the batter. Ensure the whole onion is well coated in batter, then deep-fry for 2–3 minutes, flipping over halfway to ensure both sides are golden.

7. Transfer the onion rings to a paper towel to drip off any excess oil, season with salt and serve with the aioli.

SWEET POTATO FRIES

SERVES
≪⋯1–2⋯≫

3 large sweet potatoes
(peeling optional)
2 tablespoons melted
coconut oil
salt and pepper, to taste

For the chipotle lime mayo:
3–4 tablespoons vegan
mayonnaise (store-
bought or use my recipe
on page 186)
juice of ½ lime
1–2 teaspoons chipotle chilli
paste (or more if you prefer
more of a kick)
1 tablespoon maple syrup
1 teaspoon onion powder
salt, to taste

As sweet potatoes are my favourite food, it seemed necessary
to share some fries with you all! These are super easy, delicious
and you can serve 'em up with anything you like.

1. Preheat your oven to 200°C/400°F.

2. Using a sharp knife, cut the sweet potatoes into wedges or
chips. Sweet potatoes can be quite hard to cut, so be careful and
use a good-quality knife!

3. Pop the sweet potatoes in a large bowl and massage the coconut
oil through until all the chips are coated.

4. Transfer to a baking tray lined with baking paper and bake
for approximately 40 minutes until crispy. Flip them over at the
halfway mark. (The baking time will vary depending on your
oven and how thick your chips are.)

5. Once crispy, remove from the oven, season with salt and
pepper and serve.

6. To prepare the chipotle lime mayo, simply whisk the ingredients
in a small bowl and refrigerate until ready to serve.

SECRET TIP: For super crispy chips, leave around a 1-cm
(3/4-inch) gap between each chip when placing them on the
baking tray.

TOMATO & MANGO SALSA

SERVES
≪⋯1–2⋯≫

3–4 tomatoes
1 mango (not too ripe)
a few coriander leaves
60g (½ cup) corn kernels
3 tablespoons chopped spring
    onion (green onion)
juice of 1 lime
½ teaspoon ground cumin
½ teaspoon paprika
½ teaspoon coconut sugar
¼ teaspoon salt

Enjoy this salsa with your friends, family or hog the whole bowl to yourself. I love adding it to my favourite rice dishes, salads and wraps as well! If mangoes are currently not in season, feel free to substitute with pineapple.

1. Finely dice the tomatoes and mango and finely chop the coriander leaves.

2. Combine everything in a bowl and mix well.

3. Let sit in the refrigerator for 10–15 minutes before serving to allow the flavours to merge together.

CHAPTER
5

SAUCES
&
SPREADS

CHEESY NACHO SAUCE

1 large carrot, chopped and
   boiled until soft
120g (1 cup) raw cashews,
   soaked for 3–6 hours
190ml (¾ cup) soy or
   almond milk
30g (½ cup) nutritional yeast
2 teaspoons onion powder
1 teaspoon garlic powder
½ teaspoon light miso paste
1 tablespoon lemon juice
2 teaspoons maple syrup
salt, to taste

Liquid gold. Well, liquid cheesy gold.

Blend this up, heat it up and drizzle it, pour it or drown your
food in it. It's SO delicious and so easy to make. I love pairing
this with nachos, salads, sandwiches – anything that calls for
some cheesy goodness.

1. Blend all the ingredients in a high-speed blender until smooth,
creamy and no lumps remain. To serve, simply heat up in a small
saucepan.

2. Store any leftovers in an airtight container for up to 5 days in
the refrigerator. When re-using, simply thin out the sauce with
a little plant-based milk to reach your desired consistency.

TAHINI, COCONUT
& LIME MAYO

3 tablespoons tahini
60ml (¼ cup) coconut cream
juice and zest of 1 lime
3–4 tablespoons maple syrup
   or coconut nectar
salt and pepper, to taste
1 teaspoon apple cider vinegar
   (optional)
extra coconut milk or hot
   water to thin, if needed

This tangy lil' number is perfect drizzled over your summer
salad or in wraps or sandwiches.

1. Whisk all the ingredients together with a fork until smooth.
Adjust the consistency as needed.

2. Store in an airtight jar or container in the refrigerator and
consume within 5 days.

OIL-FREE HUMMUS

SERVES
‹‹···2–3···››

1 × 400g (14oz) can chickpeas,
  rinsed and drained
2 tablespoons tahini
juice of 2 lemons
2 garlic cloves, oven-roasted
2 teaspoons ground cumin
1 tablespoon maple syrup
  or agave nectar
80ml (⅓ cup) water, plus
  more if needed
salt and pepper, to taste

I think my spirit animal is hummus. Or maybe, I'd just like to
come back as a chickpea in my next life so I can become hummus.

A lot of store-bought hummus can be laden with added oils
and preservatives, and seeing as I like to eat hummus by the
bucket load, it made a lot more sense to create a delicious, creamy,
preservative-free hummus that I can happily enjoy to my heart's
desire. (AKA – spoonfuls and spoonfuls.)

Feel free to adjust or add any spices you wish to suit your taste.

1. Blend all the ingredients in a high-speed blender or food
processor until smooth and creamy. Add more water if you'd
like a thinner consistency.

2. Store in an airtight container in the refrigerator for up to 5 days.

NOTE: A quick and easy way to roast a garlic clove is to place each
individual clove (or as many as you need) unpeeled into a preheated
oven set to 200–220°C/400–425°F and roast for 10–15 minutes.
Remove from the oven and the centre should be soft, so simply
squeeze out the delicious garlic centre and use accordingly!

PUMPKIN HUMMUS

1 × 400g (14oz) can chickpeas,
   rinsed and drained
60ml (¼ cup) tahini
150g (⅔ cup) pumpkin purée
2 garlic cloves, oven-roasted
2 teaspoons onion powder
2 teaspoons cumin
1 teaspoon paprika
2 tablespoons olive oil
1–2 tablespoons maple syrup
1 tablespoon lemon juice
salt and pepper, to taste

This savoury hummus pairs well with wraps, burgers, sandwiches, salads or as a dip on its own!

1. Place all the ingredients in a high-speed blender or food processor.

2. Slowly add a few tablespoons of water to help get the blades moving.

3. Blend or process until all lumps are gone.

4. Serve the hummus immediately or keep it in an airtight container in the refrigerator for up to 5 days.

VEGAN 'HONEY'

150g (½ cup) rice malt syrup
150g (½ cup) coconut nectar

A quick and easy method that requires only two ingredients! The sticky syrupy rice malt syrup pairs well with the caramel flavour of the coconut nectar, creating a well-balanced syrup that resembles honey and is a great base for baking, desserts and sauces. It is particularly delicious drizzled over pancakes.

1. Whisk together until well combined

2. Store in a well-sealed jar or container for up to a month at room temperature.

CREAMY VEGAN MAYONNAISE

250ml (1 cup) unrefined
    oil (sunflower, olive
    or grape seed)
160ml (½ cup plus
    2 tablespoons) soy milk
1 tablespoon maple syrup
    or rice malt syrup
1 tablespoon apple
    cider vinegar
salt to taste

Sometimes, you just want mayo. Dirty, creamy, sinful mayo. Here it is my friends.

1. Blend everything in a high-speed blender until creamy.

2. Store in an airtight container in the refrigerator for up to 7 days.

NOTE: A dense oil such as sunflower, grape seed or olive work best – it helps you achieve a really thick and creamy mayonnaise. Vegetable oil is too light and results in a very runny sauce-like consistency. This recipe is great to have on-hand to use as a base for other dressings and sauces. I normally eat every single bit of this in one go, but I can imagine, if you keep it in a sealed jar in the refrigerator, it will last for a week.

SUN-DRIED TOMATO PESTO

115g (1 cup) jarred sun-dried
    tomatoes, drained from any
    oil and rinsed under water
10–12 basil leaves
180g (1½ cups) raw cashews,
    soaked for 3–6 hours
2 garlic cloves
125ml (½ cup) extra virgin
    olive oil
80ml (¼ cup) maple syrup
1 tablespoon lemon juice
2 teaspoons nutritional yeast
salt and pepper, to taste

This creamy pesto is great as a spread, dip or as a pasta sauce! To transform this wonderful pesto into a pasta sauce, simply increase the amount of water or oil you add while blending to suit your desired consistency.

1. Pulse or blend all the ingredients in either a high-speed blender or food processor until thick and creamy. Add a little water to get the blades moving if needed.

2. Serve on bread, crackers or as a dip.

AIOLI

2 garlic cloves
2 teaspoons coconut oil
150g (1¼ cups) raw cashews,
    soaked for 3–6 hours
170ml (⅔ cup) almond milk
60ml (¼ cup) olive oil
2 teaspoons apple cider
    vinegar
2 teaspoons maple syrup
    or coconut nectar
1 teaspoon onion powder
½ teaspoon salt
¼ teaspoon black pepper

This Aioli is SO heavenly, so creamy and pairs well with any of your savoury favourites! You'll be astounded at how easy it is to make, and it stores well in the fridge. Keep this around to dip your fries in or drizzle over anything and everything. It pairs well with my Onion Rings (page 172).

A high-speed blender works best for creating delicious creamy dips and spreads, so it's definitely worth the investment.

. . . .

1. Peel and fry the garlic cloves whole in the coconut oil over a low-medium heat until golden and fragrant.

2. Rinse and drain the cashews. Blend the garlic cloves and the rest of the ingredients in a high-speed blender until smooth, creamy and no lumps remain.

3. Keep stored in an airtight container in the refrigerator for up to 5 days.

MAPLE & TAHINI MAYO

3–4 tablespoons tahini
3 tablespoons apple
    cider vinegar
juice of ½ lemon
80ml (⅓ cup) maple syrup
¼ teaspoon salt, or to taste
¼ teaspoon ground black
    pepper
hot water to thin, if needed

Two of my favourite things – maple syrup and tahini. Pair that together with some zesty lemon and apple cider vinegar, and my friends – you have one hell of a salad dressing. This also tastes great drizzled over roast vegetables... or anything, really.

. . . .

1. Whisk everything in a small bowl. Adjust the salt to taste. Add a little hot water if you'd like a thinner consistency.

2. Store in an airtight container in the refrigerator. Consume within 7 days.

WALNUT & KALE PESTO

SERVES
《··· 3–4 ···》

2 garlic cloves
1 tablespoon coconut oil
60g (½ cup) walnuts
60g (½ cup) raw cashews,
   soaked for 3–6 hours
2 large handfuls of kale leaves,
   roughly chopped
1 bunch of basil leaves
125ml (½ cup) olive oil
60ml (¼ cup) water
½ teaspoon sea salt,
   or to taste
¼ teaspoon ground black
   pepper
½ teaspoon onion powder
2 teaspoons coconut sugar
1 tablespoon nutritional yeast

This pesto is so delicious and nourishing, and it also hides a secret nutrient punch with the addition of kale! Kale is one of the most nutrient-dense plant foods; but eating it on its own is not the most enjoyable experience (it tastes a lot like chewy grass!).

I've found myriad ways to incorporate kale into my meals, and one of my favourites is hiding it in pesto. Enjoy this with salads, pasta, sandwiches and crackers or use it as a dip.

1. Fry the garlic cloves in a non-stick frying pan with the coconut oil until they brown and become fragrant.

2. Blend the garlic cloves and the rest of the ingredients in a high-speed blender or food processor until smooth and creamy.

3. Store in an airtight container and consume within 5 days.

CHEESY CHILLI QUESO DIP

SERVES
《···2–4···》

1 medium–large potato,
    peeled
1 carrot, peeled
250ml (1 cup) soy milk or
    other plant-based milk
90g (¾ cup) raw cashews,
    soaked for 3–6 hours
60ml (¼ cup) maple syrup
30g (½ cup) nutritional yeast
1 teaspoon vegetable
    stock powder
2 teaspoons onion powder
1 teaspoon garlic powder
½ teaspoon paprika
2 tablespoons tapioca starch
    or arrowroot flour
1 teaspoon chipotle chilli
    paste, or more as desired
salt, to taste
green chilli, for decoration
    (optional)

To serve:
corn chips

This is super cheesy and packs a punch. Feel free to add more chilli if you like. This pairs well with corn chips, on toasties, rice – you name it!

....

1. Dice the potato and carrot. Bring these to the boil in a medium saucepan until tender.

2. Drain and rinse under cool water.

3. Blend everything apart from the green chilli in a high-speed blender for a few minutes until smooth and silky.

4. Transfer back to a saucepan and cook over a medium heat and whisk well for a few minutes until the mixture thickens and no lumps remain.

5. Serve in a bowl, garnish with green chilli (optional), dip your corn chips in and enjoy.

MISO & GINGER DRESSING

2 tablespoons tahini
1 tablespoon almond butter
1 teaspoon light miso paste
2 teaspoons grated ginger
80ml (⅓ cup) maple syrup
    or coconut nectar
juice of 1 lemon
sea salt, to taste
hot water to thin, if needed

Ahh, miso hungry! I should probably warn you, I love a good pun. However, this Asian-inspired dressing pairs well with noodles, salad or roasted vegetables. I always have it on hand because it's a lovely addition to any dish.

1. Blend in a high-speed blender until smooth and creamy. Thin out with hot water if desired. Keep in a sealed container in the refrigerator for up to 5 days.

CASHEW CREAM

120g (1 cup) raw cashews,
    soaked for 3–6 hours
125ml (½ cup) coconut cream
80ml (⅓ cup) maple syrup or
    agave nectar
1 teaspoon pure vanilla
    extract with seeds
¼ teaspoon salt
2–3 tablespoons melted
    coconut oil or coconut
    butter
a few tablespoons water,
    if needed

This is so dangerous to have around, but I couldn't not share it with you! Save this for breakfasts, desserts… or just eat it by the spoonful. The options are endless. However, be warned – it's addictive as hell.

1. Rinse and drain your cashews.

2. Blend everything in a high-speed blender until no lumps remain. Add a little water if needed.

3. Store in an airtight container or jar in the refrigerator for up to 5 days.

MUSHROOM GRAVY

SERVES
«···1–2···»

1 brown onion, finely diced
2 garlic cloves, minced
1–2 tablespoons vegan butter
200g (3 cups) mushrooms,
    roughly chopped
1 tablespoon vegetable bouillon
    or paste (page 200)
2 teaspoons onion powder
1 teaspoon ground cumin
1 teaspoon ground nutmeg
½ teaspoon ground cloves
½ teaspoon white pepper
1 tablespoon coconut sugar
1 tablespoon tamari or
    soy sauce
175ml (¾ cup) coconut cream
1½ teaspoons cornflour
125ml (½ cup) almond milk,
    plus more if needed

I love making up big batches of this gravy and smothering my food with it in winter. It's so comforting and I know you'll love it.

· ·

1. Begin by first browning the onion and garlic in a large frying pan in the vegan butter over a medium heat.

2. Add the mushrooms to the pan along with 80ml (⅓ cup) water to prevent any sticking.

3. Add the stock powder, onion powder, spices, coconut sugar, tamari and coconut cream and simmer for 10 minutes.

4. Whisk the cornflour with the almond milk and pour this into the pan, stirring continuously.

5. Once the gravy begins to thicken, remove from the heat and serve immediately. Store in a jar or airtight container in the refrigerator for up to 5 days and reheat as necessary. (You can thin it out with liquid if needed.)

RASPBERRY & CHIA JAM

350g (1½ cups) frozen
    raspberries, thawed
125ml (½ cup) maple syrup
1 teaspoon pure vanilla
    extract with seeds
4–5 teaspoons white
    chia seeds

Chia seeds are tiny nutrient powerhouses loaded with fibre, protein, Omega-3 fatty acids and various micronutrients – so this jam rocks my world. Feel free to use any berry (or mix of berries) you like as well.

1. Mash the raspberries and maple syrup together until the raspberries have broken up slightly.

2. Stir through the vanilla and chia seeds.

3. Store in an airtight container in the refrigerator for up to a week. Allow the chia seeds to swell overnight before using the jam.

ULTIMATE VEGGIE STOCK PASTE

MAKES
《··· 3–4 ···》
CUPS

2 garlic cloves
2 brown onions
1 leek (use mainly the
    lighter end of the leek)
2 celery stalks
5 button mushrooms
2 large carrots
25–30g chopped parsley
80ml (⅓ cup) water, plus
    more if needed
80ml (⅓ cup) extra virgin
    olive oil
3–4 heaped teaspoons
    Himalayan pink salt or sea
    salt, plus more if desired
1 teaspoon miso paste
1 teaspoon onion powder
½ teaspoon ground black
    pepper
1 teaspoon dried rosemary
1 teaspoon dried thyme
1 teaspoon dried sage
2 Turkish bay leaves
½ tablespoon coconut sugar
1 tablespoon nutritional yeast
4–5 sun-dried tomatoes

No longer do you have to use MSG-laden vegetable stock powder! I love this stock paste, and always have it on hand in the kitchen. It freezes well, and can be added to any savoury dish to enhance flavour in place of traditional stock powder. A general rule of thumb is that 1–2 tablespoons of stock paste will replace 1 tablespoon of stock powder. (However, please note that this will vary depending how salty you like the stock to be.)

It's jam-packed full of vegetables and is easily adjustable to suit your taste and salt preferences. This recipe produces a slighter less salty stock, which I prefer – but please feel free to adjust this as you need.

1. Finely dice the garlic, onions, leek, celery and mushrooms. Grate the carrots. Alternatively, if you have a food processor you could chop all of the vegetables that way – however, I would recommend doing it in two batches.

2. In a large frying pan, fry the vegetables with the parsley, water and olive oil. Fry over a medium-high heat and continuously stir, adding more water if necessary to prevent sticking.

3. Once the vegetables have released their liquids and have reduced in size by half (after about 5–6 minutes), add the salt, miso paste, onion powder, pepper, herbs, coconut sugar and nutritional yeast.

4. Remove from the heat and, in a high-speed blender or food processor, blend the vegetables with the sun-dried tomatoes until smooth. Increase the speed gradually as the ingredients will be hot!

5. Allow the mixture to cool slightly before storing. Keep stored in the refrigerator in an airtight container. As this recipe makes around 750ml (3 cups)of stock paste, feel free to freeze some for later use.

SUPER RAD COCONUT 'BACON'

SERVES
2–3

2 young green coconuts,
    flesh only
80ml (⅓ cup) tamari
3 tablespoons maple syrup
3 teaspoons liquid smoke
1 teaspoon onion powder
1 teaspoon garlic powder
1 teaspoon smoked paprika
½ teaspoon sesame oil

Now, I usually make my coconut bacon simply out of coconut flakes – but if you are after its more 'meaty' counterpart, then this is for you! It's scary how much it tastes and feels like bacon. Use it in sandwiches, salads, burgers – anything that your heart desires. You could also pop this in a dehydrator for 12 hours, but I'm super impatient, so into the oven it is!

1. Scoop the flesh out of the coconuts, clean any residue or dirt off them and slice the meat into bite-sized chunks.

2. Whisk together the rest of the ingredients.

3. Sit the coconut meat and marinade in a shallow bowl for 30 minutes.

4. Preheat the oven to 180°C/350°F.

5. Line a baking tray with baking paper and bake the coconut for approximately 30–40 minutes, flipping it over halfway (bake for longer if you'd like crispier bacon, but be sure to keep an eye on it to prevent burning).

6. Store in an airtight container in the refrigerator for up to 2 weeks and serve as you need it. To reheat, simply lightly warm it in a pan or microwave.

SWEETS
&
TREATS

SPICED BANANA BREAD
WITH CHOCOLATE CHUNKS

MAKES
«··· 1 ···»
LOAF

For the wet ingredients:

4 large, very ripe bananas

175ml (⅔ cup) vegetable oil

200g (1 cup) packed
brown sugar

1 teaspoon pure vanilla
extract with seeds

For the dry ingredients:

120g (1 cup) plain
(all-purpose) flour

80g (⅔ cup) whole-wheat
flour or spelt flour

2 teaspoons baking powder

2 teaspoons ground flaxseeds

¼ teaspoon bicarbonate of
soda (baking soda)

½ teaspoon salt

1 teaspoon ground cinnamon
(optional)

1 teaspoon ground cardamom
(optional)

120g (1 scant cup) vegan
chocolate, roughly chopped

Banana bread, cakes and muffins were my absolute favourite growing up. Mum used to make me the best Banana Cake smothered in chocolate icing, and this Banana Bread brings back fond memories of that – from the moist texture, to the treasure troves of chocolate chunks. It's so delicious, and I hope your inner child enjoys this as much as mine.

1. Preheat your oven to 180°C/350°F.

2. In a large bowl, sift your dry ingredients together, apart from the chocolate.

3. In a separate bowl, mash the bananas into a purée, then add the oil, sugar and vanilla and mix well.

4. Fold the wet ingredients into the dry ones very gently then fold in the chocolate. Be sure to not over-mix!

5. Pour into a 11×21cm (4½×8½ inch) loaf tin (slightly larger than the one for Banana Bread p. 206) lined with baking paper and bake for 40–45 minutes until a toothpick comes out clean. Baking time will vary depending on your oven, so be sure to keen an eye on it!

6. Leave to cool in the tin for at least 30 minutes before turning out on to a wire rack. Leave for a further 5 minutes before slicing. Wrap any banana bread you don't manage to eat in the first sitting in cling flim and store in the refrigerator for up to 5 days.

PEANUT BUTTER
& JELLY LOAF

MAKES
《⋯ 1 ⋯》
LOAF

For the dry ingredients:
240g (2 cups) spelt or plain
    (all-purpose) flour
200g (1 cup) unrefined sugar
2 teaspoons baking powder
½ teaspoon salt
½ teaspoon ground
    cinnamon (optional,
    but recommended)

For the wet ingredients:
250ml (1 cup) soy milk
1 large, ripe banana
170ml (⅔ cup) coconut
    oil, melted
200g (1 cup) natural crunchy
    peanut butter (unsalted)
2 teaspoons pure vanilla
    extract with seeds
2 flax eggs (2 tablespoons
    ground flaxseeds mixed with
    6 tablespoons water and
    left to sit for 10 minutes)
4 heaped tablespoons
    raspberry jam

I'm not sure at what point I thought it was a good idea to make a loaf out of peanut butter and jelly (jam) – but I'm sure as hell glad I did. Best decision ever. Make it and see what I'm talking about! Feel free to substitute the raspberry jam for any flavour you like.

1. Preheat your oven to 180°C/350°F. Mix the dry ingredients in a large bowl.

2. Blend all of the wet ingredients together (except the raspberry jam) until smooth.

3. Fold the wet and dry ingredients together until a batter forms.

4. Pour the batter into a lined 900g (2 lb) loaf tin.

5. Spoon the jam onto of the top of the loaf and swirl through the batter with the back of the spoon.

6. Bake for 45–50 minutes until a toothpick comes out relatively clean. (It may take more time depending on your oven.)

7. Let it cool in the tin for 20–30 minutes before turning it out on to a wire rack. Allow to cool completely before slicing. (If you're impatient like me, just pop it in the refrigerator to help speed up the cooling process.)

8. Enjoy straight away, or keep it in an airtight container in the refrigerator for up to 5 days.

NOTE: As there will be some differences between your oven temperature and also the brand of jam you use, please ensure you keep an eye on the loaf. If the top begins to brown too fast (due to the sugar in the jam), simply reduce the oven temperature.

CHOCOLATE CAKE

SERVES
⟪⋯ 12 ⋯⟫

For the wet ingredients:
500ml (2 cups) soy milk
2 tablespoons apple
    cider vinegar
125ml (½ cup) vegetable oil
60ml (¼ cup) melted
    coconut oil
125ml (½ cup) strong
    brewed coffee
2 teaspoons vanilla bean
    powder or pure vanilla
    extract with seeds
2 flax eggs (2 tablespoons
    ground flaxseeds mixed
    with 6 tablespoons water
    and left to sit for 10 minutes)

For the dry ingredients:
300g (2½ cups) plain
    (all-purpose) flour
100g (1 cup) unsweetened
    cocoa powder
500g (2½ cups) raw cane sugar
½ teaspoon bicarbonate
    of soda (baking soda)
1 teaspoon baking powder
½ teaspoon salt
¼ teaspoon ground cinnamon

For the buttercream:
240g (2 cups) raw cashews,
    soaked for 3–6 hours
125ml (½ cup) maple syrup
60g (½ cup) cacao powder
190ml (¾ cup) plant-
    based milk
1 teaspoon pure vanilla extract
    with seeds
¼ teaspoon salt
190ml (¾ cup) melted
    coconut oil

It's always a challenge making vegan baked goods with the absence of eggs, but the two secret ingredients here – apple cider vinegar and ground coffee – produce a moist and fudgy cake that just melts in your mouth. I promise you can't taste the vinegar or the coffee! Paired with cashew chocolate buttercream, you really can't go wrong. Share this with family and friends – I promise you they won't be able to tell it's vegan!

• •

1. Preheat your oven to 180°C/350°F and grease two 20cm (8 inch) springform cake tins with coconut oil or line the bases with a circle of baking paper.

2. Combine the soy milk and apple cider vinegar and set aside.

3. Sift all of the dry ingredients into a large bowl

4. In a separate bowl, whisk together the wet ingredients, including the soy milk and apple cider vinegar.

5. Pour the wet ingredients into the dry and mix until well combined.

6. Separate the batter between the two cake tins and bake in the oven for approximately 40 minutes until a toothpick comes out clean from the centre.

7. While the cakes are baking, prepare the buttercream by rinsing and draining your cashews. Blend everything apart from the coconut oil in a high-speed blender until all lumps are gone (you may need to push it into the blades a few times as it will be thick). Add the coconut oil last and blend for another 60 seconds. Transfer the buttecream to a shallow bowl and keep it in the freezer. Remove it from the freezer every 15 minutes and whisk with a fork, whisk or electric beater to aerate and prevent any lumps forming. After whisking four times (1 hour), the buttercream should be starting to stiffen and thicken. (This time may vary depending on how cold your freezer is, so be sure to keep checking it at even intervals and use your own judgement.)

8. Set aside the buttercream in the refrigerator and once thickened allow the cakes to cool completely before icing. (If you are impatient like me, simply cool the cakes in the refrigerator.)

9. To ice the cakes, spread a thick layer of buttercream on the top of one of the cakes. Use a hot, wet butter knife to spread it evenly. Top with the second layer of cake and then being to ice the top and around the sides of the cake until evenly coated.

10. Decorate the cake with your favourite vegan chocolate (shaved), frozen raspberries and crushed pistachios.

11. Transfer the cake to the fridge, cover it and allow it to cool completely for 1–2 hours with the icing before slicing. Keep whatever you don't manage to eat straight away covered or stored in a sealed container in the refrigerator for up to 5 days. Makes 12–14 slices.

SALTED CARAMEL & CHOCOLATE BROWNIES

MAKES
«··· 6–8 ···»
SQUARES

For the dry ingredients:
150g (1½ cups) almond meal
85g (¾ cup) unsweetened
    cocoa powder or cacao
    powder
200g (1 cup) unrefined sugar
2 teaspoons baking power
½ teaspoon salt

For the wet ingredients:
125ml (½ cup) almond milk
160ml (⅔ cup) coconut oil,
    melted
2 teaspoons pure vanilla
    extract with seeds
1 × 400g (14oz) can black
    beans, rinsed and drained
1 flax egg (1 tablespoon ground
    flaxseeds mixed with
    3 tablespoons water and
    left to sit for 10 minutes)

For the salted caramel sauce:
2 tablespoons tahini
3 tablespoons maple syrup
salt, to taste

Salted caramel and chocolate are two words that are dangerous paired together!

I swear every time I make these brownies I never even get to see them all together… they are all swiftly stolen (or graciously eaten) by my friends and family. I'm not complaining, however.

You wouldn't guess it, but these brownies also pack a healthy protein punch – with the secret ingredient… beans! I promise you can't even taste them. Enjoy this brownie with the gooey salted caramel sauce, or without – either way they taste great!

1. Preheat your oven to 180°C/350°F.

2. Mix the dry ingredients in a large bowl.

3. Blend the wet ingredients (apart from the flax egg) in a high-speed blender until thick and creamy.

4. Pour this mixture into the dry ingredients and mix until all lumps are gone. Fold the flax egg mixture in last.

5. Pour into a 10×20cm (4×8 inch) loaf tin or a 20×20cm (8×8 inch) brownie tin lined with baking paper. Bake for approximately 35–40 minutes. (Keep an eye on it as I'm aware ovens can vary greatly!) Please note, the brownie will still be incredibly soft as soon as it is removed from the oven. This is a good thing, as it means it's going to be doughy and delicious.

6. Allow the brownie to cool completely before slicing by either popping it in the freezer for 10 minutes or in the refrigerator for around 30 minutes. This will allow the coconut oil to solidify and results in an incredibly delicious texture!

7. Slice your brownie into 6–8 pieces.

8. To make the caramel, simply whisk the ingredients in a small bowl until combined. Drizzle over your brownie before serving. This brownie keeps well in an airtight container in the refrigerator for up to a week.

CHOCOLATE CHIP COOKIES

MAKES
《··· 10–12 ···》
COOKIES

For the wet ingredients:
160g (1 cup) vegan butter
150g (¾ cup) soft brown
    sugar
80g (⅓ cup) unrefined sugar
2 teaspoons pure vanilla
    extract with seeds
1 tablespoon olive oil
1 flax egg (1 tablespoon
    flaxseeds mixed with
    3 tablespoons water and
    left to sit for 10 minutes)

For the dry ingredients:
200g plus 3 tablespoons
    (1⅔ cups) plain
    (all-purpose) flour
¼ teaspoon salt
½ teaspoon bicarbonate
    of soda (baking soda)
120g (1 scant cup) chopped
    vegan chocolate

A cruelty-free take on a traditional favourite of mine!
These cookies are soft, chewy and darn delicious! If you are
new to baking, and in particular cookies – a few pointers are:
• Check the best-before dates on your ingredients! In particular,
the bicarbonate of soda (baking soda).
• For best results, don't bake cookies for too long. The edges
should only be slightly golden and the centre should still be pale.
This will result in a crispy outer crust and a soft, gooey centre.
• When measuring dry ingredients (i.e. flour) it is always best
to use a spoon to distribute the ingredients into your measuring
cup as opposed to scooping straight out of the bag or tin.

1. Preheat the oven to 190°C/375°F. Beat the butter, both types
of sugar and vanilla in a large bowl using a hand mixer or electric
beater until fluffy then beat in the oil and flax egg.

2. Sift the dry ingredients into the butter mixture and fold gently.

3. When a soft dough forms, add the vegan chocolate.

4. Line a baking tray with baking paper and roll golf ball-sized
balls of cookie dough evenly around the tray – be sure to leave
at least 5–7.5cm (2–3 inches) between each cookie because
they will spread during cooking.

5. Bake for around 8–12 minutes until golden. (Adjust the time to
suit your cookie preferences i.e. a shorter time for doughy cookies
and longer time for crunchy and chewy cookies.)

6. Allow the cookies to cool slightly before transferring to a wire
rack. Store in an airtight container. They should keep for 5 days
at room temperature or 1 week refrigerated.

CHOCOLATE FUDGE BEET BROWNIES
WITH CHOCOLATE GANACHE

MAKES
6–8
SLICES

1 medium beetroot (approx. 230g), washed and chopped into small chunks
250g (1¼ cups) unrefined sugar (or sugar of choice)
125ml (½ cup) soy milk
¼ teaspoon salt
125ml (½ cup) coconut oil, melted
1 flax egg (1 tablespoon ground flaxseed mixed with 3 tablespoons water)
60g plus 4 tablespoons (½ cup) plain (all-purpose) flour
115g (1 cup) cacao powder or unsweetened cocoa powder
2 teaspoons baking powder
1 teaspoon vanilla extract

For the chocolate ganache:
1 large ripe avocado, sliced
60g (½ cup) cacao powder
125ml (½ cup) maple syrup
80ml (⅓ cup) coconut oil, melted
2 teaspoons pure vanilla extract
¼ teaspoon salt

A rich, velvety brownie laced with sweet and delicious beetroot. Beetroot provides a delicious moisture to the brownie, as well as a gorgeous crimson hue. These brownies are widely loved among my friends!

1. Preheat your oven to 180°C/350°F.

2. Blend the chopped beetroot with the sugar, soy milk, vanilla essence and salt until smooth in a high-speed blender. Add the coconut oil and flax egg last and blend once more.

3. Combine the flour, cacao powder and baking powder in a large bowl.

4. Add the wet ingredients to the dry and mix until a smooth batter forms.

5. Pour the mixture into a 20×20cm (8×8 inch) brownie pan lined with baking paper and bake for approximately 35–40 minutes. You still want the brownie to be a little moist inside as it will continue to set once removed from the oven.

6. Remove from the oven and immediately put in the refrigerator for around 30 minutes to cool before icing – this time will also allow the brownie to set further.

7. In the meantime, prepare your ganache. Blend everything in a food processor until all the avocado chunks are gone.

8. Ice the brownie and transfer to the refrigerator for another hour to allow the icing to set.

9. By this time the brownie will take on a fudgy, moist and decadent texture.

10. For best results slice with a wet knife. Enjoy straight away and keep leftovers in an airtight container in the fridge.

RASPBERRY & LEMON MUFFINS
WITH A WHITE CHOCOLATE GLAZE

MAKES
6–8
MUFFINS

For the wet ingredients:
250ml (1 cup) soy milk
2 tablespoons apple cider
    vinegar
1 flax egg (1 tablespoon ground
    flaxseeds mixed with
    3 tablespoons water and
    left to sit for 10 minutes)
150g (¾ cup) unrefined sugar
80ml (⅓ cup) vegetable oil
2 teaspoons pure vanilla
    extract with seeds

For the dry ingredients:
240g (2 cups) plain
    (all-purpose) flour
2½ teaspoons baking powder
¼ teaspoon bicarbonate
    of soda (baking soda)
¼ teaspoon salt
zest of 2 lemons

You'll also need:
100g (1 cup) frozen
    raspberries

**For the white chocolate
drizzle:**
80ml (⅓ cup) melted
    cacao butter
6 tablespoons icing sugar,
    plus more if desired
2–3 tablespoons almond milk

These muffins are perfect for school lunches, afternoon snacks or warmed up for an after dinner treat with some vegan ice-cream. The white chocolate drizzle on the top is totally optional but it is pretty damn delicious. These muffins are so easy to make, super light and fluffy and are easily adaptable. Feel free to substitute the raspberries with any fruit or berries of your choice.

1. Preheat your oven to 170°C/325°F and line a muffin tray with muffin cases or squares of baking paper.

2. Mix the soy milk and apple cider vinegar together and set aside to thicken.

3. Sift your dry ingredients together into a large bowl.

4. In a separate bowl, whisk together the soy milk and vinegar mixture, the flax egg, the sugar and the rest of the wet ingredients until well combined.

5. Gently fold the wet ingredients into the dry, but be careful not to over mix – you want it to be well combined but a few lumps are fine! Fold in the raspberries.

6. Fill the muffin trays so they are around three-quarters full.

7. Bake for 35 minutes (longer if needed) until a toothpick comes out clean and they are slightly golden on top.

8. Allow them to cool in the pan for around 10 minutes before transferring to a wire rack.

9. To prepare the white chocolate drizzle, simply whisk the ingredients in a small bowl. Add more icing sugar or almond milk as necessary to reach your desired consistency.

10. Drizzle over the muffins and enjoy! Keep any leftover muffins, sealed, in a cool, dry place. They should keep for 3–5 days.

CHAPTER
7

RAW
DESSERTS

PEANUT CARAMEL
COOKIE CHEESECAKE

For the base:

130g (1 cup) raw almonds
75g (1 cup) coconut flakes
¼ teaspoon ground cinnamon
pinch of salt
240g or 12 large pitted
    Medjool dates
1 tablespoon coconut oil

For the caramel:

200g or 10 pitted Medjool
    dates, soaked in boiling
    water for 15 minutes
125ml (½ cup) maple syrup
1 tablespoon almond butter
1 tablespoon natural
    peanut butter
1 teaspoon vanilla bean paste
½ teaspoon pink salt

1 tablespoon coconut butter
or coconut oil

For the cheesecake:

420g (3½ cups) raw cashews,
    soaked for 3–6 hours
250ml (1 cup) maple syrup
250ml (1 cup) almond milk
2 teaspoons vanilla bean paste
¼ teaspoon ground cinnamon
2 heaped tablespoons natural
    peanut butter
6–8 tablespoons coconut
    butter**
250ml (1 cup) melted coconut
    oil
1 tablespoon cacao powder

1. To make the base, pulse or blend the almonds, coconut flakes, cinnamon and salt in a high-speed blender or food processor until a fine meal forms. Add the dates and coconut oil and continue to blend until it begins to stick together into a dough. Wet your hands if necessary and press evenly into a 20–22cm springform cake tin and freeze.

2. Prepare the caramel by draining and blending the dates with the remaining caramel ingredients and set aside.

3. For the cheesecake, simply blend all the cheesecake ingredients apart from the coconut butter, coconut oil and cacao powder in a high-speed blender or food processor until smooth and creamy. Add the coconut oil and butter last and continue to blend until no lumps remain. Add more liquid if needed. Do not add the cacao powder just yet!

4. To prepare the cheesecake, pour the majority of the cheesecake mixture on to the base, reserving approximately ⅔ cup in the blender. Set this aside. Now, take the caramel you prepared earlier and place tablespoon-sized chunks around the mixture, pressing it into the centre. Feel free to set a small amount aside to decorate the cake with at step 8.

5. Take the ⅔ cup of mixture you reserved in the blender and quickly blitz it with the cacao powder until well combined. Spoon this mixture randomly around the cake until the cheesecake tin is full. Any leftover can be stored in a resealable bag and refrigerated to decorate the cake the next day.

6. Now, using a spatula, swirl the mixture around and flatten the top of the cake. This will give it a chocolate 'marbled' effect. Give the cake tin a shake to help flatten out any air bubbles or lumps. Freeze the whole cake overnight. This will need 20 minutes to defrost later.

For the peanut butter balls
60g (½ cup) raw cashews
65g (½ cup) raw almonds
35g (½ cup) coconut flakes
¼ teaspoon ground cinnamon
pinch of salt
200g or 10 Medjool dates,
    pitted
1 tablespoon maple syrup
1 heaped tablespoon peanut
    butter
1 tablespoon cacao powder

To decorate (optional):
Chocolate Drizzle (page 227)
Vegan Snickers Bars (page 246)
dehydrated orange or
    blood orange
raw or roasted peanuts
vegan white chocolate

7. To make the Peanut Butter Balls for decorating, simply blend the cashews, almonds, coconut flakes, cinnamon and salt in a food processor into a coarse meal. Add the remaining ingredients apart from the cacao powder and blend until it sticks together into a dough. Split the mixture into two and with your hands mix the cacao powder into one half of the mixture. Roll each mixture into your desired-sized balls and set aside in the refrigerator until ready to decorate.

8. To serve and decorate, allow the cake to sit for 5 minutes before removing from the tin. Decorate with the chocolate drizzle, the peanut butter balls, Vegan Snickers Bars and pipe any leftover cheesecake or caramel filling that you reserved at steps 4 and 5.

9. Allow the cake to sit for a further 30 minutes at room temperature before slicing with a sharp, hot knife. Any uneaten slices can be stored in the freezer for up to a month.

** Make your own coconut butter by blending 3–4 cups of desiccated coconut in a food processor for 5–10 minutes until it becomes a smooth paste. Store at room temperature in a sealed jar.

RAW CHOCOLATE
MINT CHEESECAKE SLICES

MAKES
《··· 6–8 ···》
PIECES

For the base:
130g (1 cup) raw almonds
75g (1 cup) coconut flakes
3 tablespoons cacao powder
240g or 12 large pitted
    Medjool dates
1 tablespoon maple syrup

For the mint layer:
120g (1 cup) raw cashews,
    soaked for 3–6 hours
2 drops good-quality food-
    grade peppermint oil
125ml (½ cup) almond milk
125ml (½ cup) rice malt
    syrup
1 teaspoon matcha powder
    or green spirulina powder
1 teaspoon vanilla powder
80ml (⅓ cup) melted
    coconut oil

**For the chocolate
mousse layer:**
240g (2 cups) raw cashews,
    soaked for 3–6 hours
175ml (⅔ cup) maple syrup
125ml (½ cup) water,
    plus more if needed
35g (⅓ cup) cacao powder
1 teaspoon vanilla powder
80ml (⅓ cup) melted
    coconut oil

This is a winner among my friends, boyfriend and family as well. It gets me every time. The chocolate brownie base paired with the freshness of the mint layer, and oh – did I mention the chocolate mousse layer on top?! Oh yeah, it's heaven. It's super simple to make, and if you are new to raw desserts, I highly recommend you give this a try!

Investing in a good blender (in my honest opinion) is paramount to making successful raw desserts – it will allow you to achieve the perfect texture!

1. Prepare the base first by pulsing the almonds, coconut and cacao in a food processor until a fine meal forms. Add the dates and maple syrup, and continue to blend until it begins to stick together like a dough. If it's too dry, add a little water. Press this evenly into a lined 10×20cm (4×8 inch) loaf tin.

2. To make the mint layer, simply blend everything apart from the coconut oil in a food processor or high-speed blender until no cashew lumps remain. Add the coconut oil last and blend for another 60 seconds. Pour over the base and freeze for around 2–3 hours until the mint layer is firm to the touch.

3. Prepare the chocolate mousse layer by blending everything apart from the coconut oil in a food processor or high-speed blender until no lumps remain. Add the coconut oil last and once it has fully blended, pour over the mint layer. Freeze the whole slice for another 4–5 hours or ideally overnight.

4. Remove from the freezer and defrost for 20 minutes before cutting with a hot knife into your desired sizes. I would advise letting the slice sit for 10 minutes prior to cuting to allow it to soften.

For the chocolate drizzle:

80ml (⅓ cup) melted
    coconut oil
2 tablespoons cacao powder
1 tablespoon agave or
    maple syrup
pinch of salt

To decorate:

crushed pistachios
mint leaves

5. To make the chocolate drizzle, simply whisk the ingredients together in a bowl and drizzle over the slice.

6. Keep these stored in the freezer. However, these slices are best consumed if left for around 10 minutes to defrost – this will allow them to soften and take on a more 'cheesecake'-like texture.

RAW VEGAN CARROT CAKE
WITH CASHEW CREAM CHEESE FROSTING

MAKES
1
CAKE

90g (1 cup) wholegrain oats
130g (1 cup) raw almonds
60g (½ cup) coconut flour
4 tablespoons ground flaxseed
1 tablespoon psyillium husks
240g or 12 large pitted
    Medjool dates
3 large carrots, peeled and
    cut into small pieces
½ teaspoon ground cloves
½ teaspoon ground nutmeg
½ teaspoon ground cinnamon
¼ teaspoon salt
½ teaspoon vanilla powder
2 tablespoons coconut sugar
2 tablespoons coconut oil
water, if needed

**For the cashew cream
cheese frosting:**
120g (1 cup) raw cashews,
    soaked for 3–6 hours
125ml (½ cup) coconut cream
80ml (⅓ cup) maple syrup
1 teaspoon pure vanilla
    extract with seeds
1 tablespoon lemon juice
2–3 tablespoons soft
    coconut oil

When I first tried this cake, I couldn't believe it was raw! It has such a light, 'cake-like' texture unlike other raw cakes I've tried. This is a great, light afternoon snack and will leave you feeling energised with the wide variety of whole foods it contains.

1. In a food processor or high-speed blender, blend the oats and almonds until a fine meal forms.

2. Add the rest of the ingredients and blend until the carrots have fully broken up into a meal. It should be a light yet dense, moist texture that holds together. Add a little water if it's too dry. (NOTE: When using a high-speed blender, make sure you use the tamping tool to press the mixture towards the blades. Alternatively, for a food processor, simply scrape down the sides of the bowl.)

3. Press firmly and evenly into a 10×20cm (4×8 inch) loaf tin lined with baking paper.

4. Freeze for 45 minutes.

5. To make the frosting, blend everything except the coconut oil in a high-speed blender until no lumps remain. Add the coconut oil last, blend again and pour over the carrot cake. Freeze for a further 30 minutes before slicing.

6. Keep the cake stored in the refrigerator in an airtight container.

NOTE: This cake holds well in the refrigerator for around a day or two. If you want to keep it for longer, simply freeze it and defrost prior to consuming.

SALTED CARAMEL SLICE

MAKES
6–8
SLICES

For the base:
130g (1 cup) raw almonds
75g (1 cup) desiccated coconut
240g or 12 large pitted
    Medjool dates
⅛ teaspoon salt

For the salted caramel:
200g (2 cups) tahini
375ml (1½ cups) maple syrup
80ml (⅓ cup) rice malt syrup
2 teaspoons vanilla powder
    or pure vanilla extract
    with seeds
Himalayan pink salt to taste
    (start with 1 teaspoon
    and add more to taste)
125ml (½ cup) melted
    coconut oil

For the chocolate:
125ml (½ cup) melted
    coconut oil
50g (½ cup) cacao powder
60ml (¼ cup) maple syrup
pinch of salt

This is hands down THE BEST caramel slice recipe you will ever lay your eyes on.

Not to mention, it's super easy! This is seriously a crowd pleaser, and I'm so excited to share it with you. The combination of maple syrup and rice malt syrup is essential to achieving a firm caramel (i.e. one that doesn't turn into a gloopy mess!), and you better get your good mixing arm ready because this caramel needs a good ol' whip.

1. To make the base, simply pulse the almonds and coconut in a food processor until a fine meal forms. Add the dates and salt and pulse until it begins to clump together into a dough. Add water, if needed.

2. Press into a 10×20cm (4×8 inch) lined loaf tin and freeze. Wet your hands to prevent it sticking or crumbling.

3. To make the caramel, in a large mixing bowl combine the tahini, maple syrup, rice malt syrup, vanilla and salt. Beat vigorously with a spatula for around 3–4 minutes until it begins to thicken.

4. Add the coconut oil and slowly combine. Beat for another 3–5 minutes until the mixture continues to thicken even more. Pour the caramel over the base and freeze for 30 minutes.

5. Whisk together the chocolate ingredients until smooth. Set this aside to cool for 15 minutes. Give it another quick whisk and then pour over the slice and freeze the whole slice overnight or for at least 6 hours. (Letting the chocolate sit at room temperature will reduce any cracks forming on the slice.)

6. When ready to slice, slice with a hot, wet and sharp knife. Keep pieces stored in the freezer and defrost for 10–15 minutes prior to devouring.

PEANUT BUTTER
& JELLY SLICE

MAKES
≪⋯ 6–8 ⋯≫
SLICES

For the base:
130g (1 cup) almonds
75g (1 cup) coconut flakes
pinch of ground cinnamon
    (optional)
pinch of salt
240g or 12 large pitted
    Medjool dates

For the peanut cream:
300g (2½ cups) raw cashews,
    soaked for 3–6 hours
250ml (1 cup) almond milk
2–3 teaspoons pure vanilla
    extract with seeds
190ml (¾ cup) maple syrup
¼ teaspoon salt
150g (⅔ cup) natural
    peanut butter
125ml (½ cup) melted
    coconut oil

For the raspberry jam layer:
125ml (½ cup) maple syrup
1 teaspoon chia seeds
150g (1½ cups) frozen
    raspberries
125ml (½ cup) melted
    coconut oil

Seriously, this combo never ceases to amaze me and this slice truly is amazing! The secret to a really creamy slice is to ensure you blend the cashews really well before adding any coconut oil. This is one of my most cherished recipes – mainly because of its simplicity and how damn delicious it tastes.

1. To make the base, simply pulse the almonds and coconut flakes in a food processor until a fine meal forms. Add the cinnamon, salt and dates and continue to pulse until it begins to stick together forming a dough. Press it into a lined 10×20cm (4×8 inch) loaf tin and freeze.

2. To make the peanut cream, blend the soaked cashews, almond milk, vanilla, maple syrup, salt and peanut butter in a high-speed blender or food processor until thick and creamy. There should be no lumps! Add the coconut oil last and continue to blend for a further 30 seconds. If you are using a blender and the blender is having a hard time with the mixture, add a little water and use a tamping stick to help the mixture spin around the blades. Pour on top of the base and freeze for 2–3 hours.

3. Prepare your raspberry layer by simply blending the maple syrup, chia seeds and raspberries in a high-speed blender until smooth. Add the coconut oil last. Pour over the frozen peanut layer and freeze again for around 1–2 hours.

NOTE: Ideally, you can leave this slice overnight to set but it should be frozen for at least 4 hours before slicing. For best results, slice with a hot, wet knife and keep the slice stored either in the fridge or freezer in an airtight container. If frozen, defrost it for at least 10–12 minutes before consuming – this gives it a chance to reach a really nice soft cheesecake-like texture.

PUMPKIN PIE CHEESECAKE SLICE

MAKES
«··· 6–8 ···»
SLICES

For the base:
65g (½ cup) raw almonds
60g (½ cup) raw pecans
75g (1 cup) desiccated coconut
240g or 12 large pitted
    Medjool dates
2 teaspoons maple syrup
½ teaspoon salt

For the filling:
240g (2 cups) raw cashews,
    soaked for 3–6 hours
375ml (1½ cups) pumpkin
    purée
190ml (¾ cup) maple syrup
125ml (½ cup) coconut cream
2–3 teaspoons pure vanilla
    extract with seeds
1½ teaspoons ground
    cinnamon, plus more
    to taste
½ teaspoon allspice,
    plus more to taste
125ml (½ cup) melted
    coconut oil

For the cashew cream:
120g (1 cup) raw cashews,
    soaked for 3–6 hours
125ml (½ cup) coconut cream
80ml (⅓ cup) maple syrup
    or agave nectar
1 teaspoon pure vanilla
    extract with seeds
¼ teaspoon salt
2–3 tablespoons soft
    coconut oil

An American friend of mine named Angie once made an EPIC pumpkin pie, and I've been trying to recreate an (almost) raw vegan version ever since, and I was super happy with the results.

This slice is like eating pumpkin pie in ice-cream form – and that's a form I'm very happy about.

Although it's not 100% raw (cue the raw police) – it still has the delicious texture and taste that raw cheesecakes are well known for. Enjoy!

1. To make the base, simply pulse the almonds, pecans and coconut in a food processor until a fine meal forms. Add the dates, maple syrup and salt, and pulse until the mixture begins to stick together in clumps. Add more dates if it is not sticking together. Press it into a 20×20cm (8×8 inch) dish lined with baking paper and freeze while you make the filling.

2. To make the filling, simply blend all the ingredients in a high-speed blender (apart from the coconut oil) until smooth and all the lumps are gone. Give it a taste and adjust the spices to suit.

3. Add the coconut oil last and blend for a further 30 seconds.

4. Pour the mixture over the base and freeze for 4 or more hours or ideally overnight until the slice is completely frozen.

5. For the cashew cream, simply blend all ingredients in a high-speed blender until thick and creamy. Keep chilled in the refrigerator until the slice has frozen.

6. Once the slice has frozen, allow the slice to defrost for 10 minutes and slice with a hot, wet knife for best results. Pipe with cashew cream, a dusting of cinnamon and enjoy immediately. Keep any leftover slices stored in the freezer and defrost as you need them. Keep any leftover cashew cream stored in a sealed container in the refrigerator and consume within 3–4 days.

COOKIES & CREAM
CHEESECAKE SLICE

MAKES
«··· 6–8 ···»
PIECES

**For the base and
cookie pieces:**
130g (1 cup) raw almonds
90g (1 cup) wholegrain oats
   (or coconut flakes)
50g (½ cup) cacao powder
½ teaspoon vanilla powder
½ teaspoon salt
320g or 16 large pitted
   Medjool dates

For the cream filling:
300g (2½ cups) raw cashews,
   soaked for 3–6 hours
250ml (1 cup) coconut cream
80ml (⅓ cup) maple syrup
125ml (½ cup) rice malt syrup
80ml (⅓ cup) water
2–3 teaspoons vanilla powder
   or pure vanilla extract
   with seeds
125ml (½ cup) melted
   coconut oil

There's something about cookies and cream that just gets me, every time. Maybe it's the cookies, maybe it's the cream. The moist, chocolate, fudge-like cookie paired with that sweet, velvety cream honestly rocks my tastebuds – and I'm so excited to share this recipe with you. This little sweetheart has been a long-time favourite of mine, and those close to me will agree! (It's a common theme for everyone leaving my house to carry takeaway containers full of tasty treats like this to take home.) I hope you enjoy making this, just as much as you will definitely enjoy eating it.

1. Begin by pulsing the almonds, oats, cacao powder, vanilla powder and salt in a food processor until a fine meal forms. Add the dates and continue to pulse until the mixture begins to stick together and forms a dough. Add a little water if it's too dry. Reserve one-third of the mixture and set aside – this will be for the 'cookie pieces'.

2. Press the base into a 10×20cm (4×8 inch) lined loaf tin or medium springform cake tin and freeze.

3. To make the filling, drain and blend the cashews with coconut cream, maple and rice malt syrups, water and vanilla powder until thick and no lumps of cashews remain. Add the coconut oil last and continue to blend for 30 seconds. Pour over the base.

4. Using the base mixture that you set aside, roll it into small 'clumps' or balls and gently press them into the cream filling. Smooth the top with a knife.

5. Freeze the whole slice ideally overnight or for at least 4–5 hours.

6. Slice with a hot, wet knife for best results. Allow the slice to defrost for 10–15 minutes before consuming. Keep stored in the refrigerator until you are ready to serve or freeze for longer-term storage. Simply defrost individual pieces as you need them.

RASPBERRY & WHITE CHOCOLATE SLICE

MAKES
《⋯ **6–8** ⋯》
PIECES

For the base:
130g (1 cup) raw almonds
75g (1 cup) coconut flakes
½ teaspoon salt
240g or 12 large pitted
    Medjool dates

For the filling:
300g (2½ cups) raw cashews,
    soaked for 3–6 hours
190ml (¾ cup) coconut milk
125ml (½ cup) maple syrup
    or rice malt syrup
125ml (½ cup) water
2 teaspoons pure vanilla
    extract with seeds
80ml (⅓ cup) melted
    cacao butter
80ml (⅓ cup) melted
    coconut oil
100g (1 cup) frozen
    raspberries

This slice is super easy and 100% delicious. If you've never used cacao butter before, you usually buy it in blocks or chunks. It can be a little more expensive than coconut oil, but cacao butter is what will give this slice a rich 'white chocolate' taste. To melt cacao butter, simply finely chop or grate the cacao butter and melt it in a small heatproof bowl over a pot of gently simmering water.

1. To make the base, simply pulse the almonds, coconut flakes and salt in a food processor until a fine meal forms. Add the dates and process until it begins to stick together into a dough. Press into a lined 10×20cm (4×8 inch) loaf tin and freeze.

2. Drain and rinse the cashews. Blend them with the coconut milk, maple syrup, water and vanilla in a high-speed blender until no lumps remain. Keep blending and slowly add the cacao butter and coconut oil.

3. Pour over the base. Disperse frozen raspberries evenly throughout the slice and then smooth the top.

4. Freeze the whole slice for 3–4 hours or ideally overnight until fully frozen.

5. To serve, allow the slice to defrost for at least 15 minutes before cutting with a hot, wet knife.

6. Keep stored in a sealed container in the freezer and simply defrost slices prior to consuming.

LEMON & COCONUT CHEESECAKE

MAKES
1
CHEESECAKE

For the base:
75g (1 cup) coconut flakes
130g (1 cup) raw almonds
½ teaspoon salt
240g or 12 large pitted
    Medjool dates
water, if needed

For the lemon filling:
360g (3 cups) raw cashews,
    soaked for 3–6 hours
zest of 4 lemons
juice of 2 lemons
2 teaspoons vanilla powder
½ teaspoon ground turmeric
    (for colour)
175ml (⅔ cup) coconut cream
190ml (¾ cup) pure
    maple syrup
125ml (½ cup) water
175ml (⅔ cup) melted
    coconut oil

For the coconut topping:
120g (1 cup) raw cashews,
    soaked for 3–6 hours
175ml (⅔ cup) coconut cream
80ml (⅓ cup) maple syrup
    or rice malt syrup
125ml (½ cup) water
½ teaspoon vanilla powder
80ml (⅓ cup) melted
    coconut oil

To decorate:
lemon slices or zest
coconut flakes or desiccated
    coconut
frozen or fresh raspberries
crushed pistachios
black sesame seeds

This summery cake is perfect for celebrations! I love using lemon in raw desserts because it resembles some kind of delicious lemon cream pie. This cake is really easy to make, and feel free to scale the quantities up or down to suit the desired cake size you are after.

1. Prepare the base by pulsing the coconut flakes, almonds and salt in a food processor until a fine meal forms. Add the Medjool dates and process further until a dough begins to stick together. Press into a lined 20–23cm (6–8 inch) springform cake tin then freeze. (I like to line just the base of the cake tin with baking paper, as it allows for easy removal.)

2. For the lemon filling, begin draining and rinsing the cashews. Pop them in a high-speed blender with the lemon zest, juice, vanilla, turmeric, coconut cream, maple syrup and water. Blend on a high speed until there are no lumps and the mixture is smooth and creamy. (A tamper tool for your blender comes in handy at this stage to help the mixture circulate around the blades.)

3. Add the coconut oil last, and blend further until the mixture is smooth and silky. Pour over the base evenly and freeze for at least 3–4 hours until firm to the touch.

4. For the coconut topping, blend the cashews, coconut cream, maple syrup, water and vanilla until smooth and creamy. Add the coconut oil last and blend for a further 60 seconds. Pour over the lemon layer and freeze the whole cake overnight.

5. When ready to serve, allow the cake to defrost for 5–10 minutes before removing it from the tin. For best slicing results, let it defrost for 20 minutes before slicing with a hot, wet and sharp knife. Decorate the cake however you'd like from suggestions listed.

6. Keep any leftover cheesecake stored in the freezer and simply defrost slices for 15–20 minutes prior to consuming.

GINGER SLICE

MAKES
⟪⋯ 6–8 ⋯⟫
SLICES

For the base:
140g (1½ cups)
  wholegrain oats
75g (1 cup) coconut flakes
240g or 12 large pitted
  Medjool dates
1 tablespoon melted
  coconut oil
1 teaspoon ground ginger
½ teaspoon salt

For the ginger filling:
120g (1 cup) raw cashews,
  soaked for 3–6 hours
250ml (1 cup) maple syrup
  or rice malt syrup
3 teaspoons ground ginger
1 teaspoon vanilla powder
175ml (⅔ cup) melted
  coconut oil

Ginger slice is an old, Kiwi classic. I remember eating my body weight in the stuff as a child back in New Zealand. However, it had been so long since I last had a piece that I almost forgot what it tasted like. I had a strong craving for it not too long ago, and thought it was a great chance to recreate my childhood favourite into a wholesome, raw vegan version – and I honestly feel like it's even more delicious than the classic. And the bonus – I don't feel sick after eating it! You won't find any refined sugars or butter in here, just wholesome plant foods.

1. Begin by pulsing the oats and coconut in a food processor until a fine meal forms (ensure all of the oats have blended). Add the Medjool dates, coconut oil, ginger and salt and continue to pulse until it begins to stick like a dough. Add a little water if it's too crumbly. Press this into a lined 10×20cm (4×8 inch) loaf tin and place in the freezer.

2. While the base is freezing, prepare your ginger filling by simply draining then blending the soaked cashews with the maple syrup, ginger and vanilla until creamy and all the cashew lumps are gone. Add the coconut oil last and blend for a further 30 seconds. Pour this mixture over the base and freeze for at least 3–4 hours or until set.

3. Slice with a hot, wet knife. Enjoy immediately or keep the slice stored in the freezer and simply defrost it for around 10 minutes prior to eating. Enjoy!

ESPRESSO BARS

MAKES
《··· 6–8 ···》
PIECES

For the brownie base:
130g (1 cup) raw almonds
2 tablespoons cacao powder
2 tablespoons coconut flour
60g (¾ cup) coconut flakes
½ teaspoon salt
240g or 12 large pitted
    Medjool dates

For the espresso layer:
240g (2 cups) cashews,
    soaked for 3–6 hours
80ml (⅓ cup) strong espresso
    or brewed coffee
175ml (⅔ cup) maple syrup
2 teaspoons vanilla powder
125ml (½ cup) almond milk,
    plus more if needed
125ml (½ cup) melted
    coconut oil

For the vanilla cream layer:
120g (1 cup) cashews, soaked
    for 3–6 hours
175ml (⅔ cup) coconut cream
125ml (½ cup) rice malt
    syrup or maple syrup
1 teaspoon vanilla powder
80ml (⅓ cup) melted
    coconut oil

A simple (mostly) raw vegan take on tiramisu! I'm an avid coffee drinker (I probably shouldn't as it doesn't do wonders for my anxiety but I do love the taste). Mum used to make an AMAZING baked coffee cake when I was younger... and it was literally just a moist cake that tasted like coffee. However, lots of sugar, butter and coffee swimming around in an 8-year-old's system probably wasn't (and isn't) the best of ideas (sorry Mum!). So here's my take on Mum's recipe – minus the refined sugar, butter and nasties.

1. Prepare the brownie base by pulsing the almonds, cacao powder, coconut flour, coconut flakes and salt in a food processor until a fine meal forms. Add the dates and process until it forms a dough, adding 1–2 tablespoons water if needed.

2. Press into a lined 10×20cm (4×8 inch) loaf tin and freeze.

3. For the espresso layer, rinse and drain your cashews. Blend in a high-speed blender with the coffee, maple syrup, vanilla and almond milk until thick and creamy and no lumps of cashews remain. Add a little more almond milk if you need to. Add the coconut oil last and continue to blend until smooth. Pour over the base evenly and freeze for 2–3 hours until firm.

4. Once the espresso layer is firm, finish with the vanilla cream layer. Once again, drain and rinse the cashews. Blend with the coconut cream, rice malt syrup and vanilla until silky smooth. Add the coconut oil last and blend again. Pour over the espresso layer and freeze the whole slice for 4–5 hours or ideally overnight.

5. When ready to serve, allow it to sit at room temperature for 10–15 minutes before slicing with a hot, wet knife. Enjoy immediately and keep any leftover pieces stored in the freezer – simply defrost as you need.

RAW 'SNICKERS' BARS

MAKES
≪⋯ **6–8** ⋯≫
BARS

For the nougat base:
90g (1 cup) wholegrain oats
60g (½ cup) coconut flour
2 tablespoons rice malt syrup
1 tablespoon soft coconut oil
   or coconut butter
¼ teaspoon salt
60ml (¼ cup) almond milk,
   plus more if needed

For the caramel:
240g or 12 large pitted
   Medjool dates, soaked for
   10 minutes in boiling water
2 tablespoons almond butter
1 tablespoon tahini
80ml (⅓ cup) melted
   coconut oil
60ml (¼ cup) maple syrup
1 teaspoon pure vanilla
   extract with seeds
½ teaspoon salt
130g (1 cup) unsalted roasted
   or raw peanuts

For the chocolate coating:
100g (1 cup) cacao powder
   or cocoa powder
200ml (¾ cup) melted
   cacao butter
80ml (⅓ cup) pure maple
   syrup
¼ teaspoon salt

I think these lil' guys speak for themselves.

Although there are a few steps to follow, it's definitely worth it – these bars are so delicious, and taste like the real deal. I will also point out that for the chocolate coating, I have stated to use either cacao powder or cocoa powder. This is totally down to your taste preferences – cacao has a strong, bitter taste to it, whereas cocoa powder is a little more subtle and rich.

Anyway, these are great to have stored in your freezer for those emergency sweet tooth attacks.

Disclaimer: If you choose the cocoa powder and the roasted peanut route, these will not be 100% raw, so I will leave this up to your preference. Personally, I prefer the taste of roasted peanuts over raw ones – so I usually always swing that way.

⋯⋯⋯⋯⋯⋯⋯⋯⋯⋯⋯⋯⋯⋯⋯⋯⋯⋯⋯⋯⋯⋯⋯⋯

1. Begin by blending the oats and coconut flour in a high-speed blender or food processor until it forms a fine meal. Transfer it to a mixing bowl.

2. Mix in the rice malt, coconut oil or butter and salt into the meal and add the almond milk. Add an extra few tablespoons at a time until it begins to come together into a soft dough. Press the dough into a lined 10×20cm (4×8 inch) loaf tin and pop it in the freezer whilst you make the caramel. A handy tip is to wet your hands whilst pressing it down – this will avoid any cracks forming and allow you to get a really nice smooth layer.

3. To make the caramel, first drain the dates, and blend them in a high-speed blender or food processor with the almond butter, tahini, coconut oil, maple syrup, vanilla extract and salt (leave the peanuts out) until smooth and creamy. Add water if needed.

4. Transfer the caramel to a small bowl and stir the peanuts through it. Spread the caramel and peanut mixture over the base evenly and put back in the freezer. Freeze for at least 3–4 hours before slicing.

5. Prepare the chocolate by sift the cocoa or cacao powder into the liquid ingredients, then whisking everything together until well combined. (If you need to melt your cacao butter first, simply melt it in a heatproof bowl over a pan of gently simmering water.) Transfer this to a shallow bowl that is large enough for you to dip your snickers into.

6. Slice the snickers widthways so you are left with 6–8 evenly sized bars. Trim the edges a little with a sharp knife.

7. Gently dip and coat each snickers in the chocolate and transfer them to a board lined with baking paper. Dip each bar twice in chocolate until well coated. Ensure the board will fit into the freezer and transfer them back to the freezer for a few minutes to set the chocolate before consuming.

8. Keep any leftover bars stored in an airtight container in the freezer and defrost a little before eating. Enjoy!

CHAPTER
8

SMOOTHIES
&
BEVERAGES

SMOOTHIE TIPS TO SUCCESS:

···· **1** ····

Freeze your bananas the night before by peeling them and storing
them in an airtight container. Ripe, spotty bananas are best!

···· **2** ····

Break the frozen bananas into chunks before blending to make
it easier to blend.

···· **3** ····

Feel free to adjust the liquid ratios to suit your desired consistency
(i.e. less liquid for a thicker, 'ice-cream' texture or more liquid for
a thinner smoothie)

···· **4** ····

Substitute any sugars or sweeteners to suit your dietary
preferences

···· **5** ····

I like my smoothies large and sweet, but feel free to use
less bananas or less liquid if desired and adjust to suit your
own dietary requirements.

50 SHADES OF GREEN

MAKES
1
SMOOTHIE

For the white layer:

1 frozen banana, broken
  into chunks
125ml (½ cup) water
125ml (½ cup) coconut milk
1 tablespoon maple syrup
1 teaspoon vanilla powder

For the green layer:

2 frozen bananas, broken
  into chunks
250ml (1 cup) almond milk
125ml (½ cup) coconut
  water or water
2 large handfuls of kale,
  stemmed and roughly
  chopped
1 large handful of spinach
  leaves
1 teaspoon green spirulina
  powder or matcha powder
4 large Medjool dates, pitted
1 tablespoon almond butter
juice of ½ lemon

It's green, sexy and delicious. I was getting a bit bored with my conventional plain green smoothie, so I thought what better way to mix things up than to go a little crazy with the colours – or in this case, shades! Feel free to incorporate any of your favourite greens – but please, don't skimp on the almond butter! It makes everything taste better.

1. Begin by blending the ingredients for the white smoothie layer in a high-speed blender until smooth and creamy. Transfer it to a tall jar or glass and set aside.

2. Blend the green layer ingredients in the same blender (no need to worry about washing the jug) until smooth and creamy.

3. To assemble, find a large glass jar and alternate between pouring or spooning in layers of green and white.

4. Slurp and enjoy!

APPLE PIE SMOOTHIE

MAKES
1
SMOOTHIE

For the raw-nola layer:
45g (½ cup) wholegrain oats
40g (½ cup) coconut flakes
½ teaspoon ground cinnamon
pinch of salt
80g or 4 large Medjool
    dates, pitted

For the smoothie:
2 frozen bananas, broken
    into chunks
2 green apples, peeled
    and cored
250ml (1 cup) oat, rice
    or almond milk
125ml (½ cup) water
3 tablespoons coconut sugar
1 teaspoon ground cinnamon
1 teaspoon ground cardamom
½ teaspoon ground cloves
1 teaspoon pure vanilla
    powder

To serve:
apple slices
ground cinnamon, for dusting

There seems to be this thing where I turn my favourite desserts into smoothies. I mean, what better way to enjoy breakfast – right? This smoothie is so incredibly delicious. The warm spices paired with the creamy, frozen banana take things to another level. Enjoy this for breakfast, or even as a healthy dessert.

1. Begin by preparing your raw-nola by pulsing the oats and coconut flakes, cinnamon and salt in a high-speed blender or food processor until a fine crumb forms. Add the dates and process until it begins to crumb together a little. Set aside.

2. Blend your smoothie ingredients in a high-speed blender until smooth and creamy.

3. Serve in a jar and alternate by layering the raw-nola and smoothie layers until you have used all your mixture. Finish with a layer of raw-nola.

4. Decorate with sliced apple and a dust of cinnamon. This is best eaten with a spoon or thick straw to enjoy the gooey raw-nola chunks.

BOUNTY SMOOTHIE

MAKES
1
SMOOTHIE

For the smoothie:
2 frozen bananas, broken
    into chunks
125ml (½ cup) coconut
    milk or cream
250ml (1 cup) fresh young
    coconut water
40g (½ cup) desiccated
    coconut, plus extra
    to decorate (optional)
3 tablespoons rice malt syrup
    or maple syrup
1 teaspoon pure vanilla powder

For the ganache:
60ml (¼ cup) maple syrup
60ml (¼ cup) coconut cream
2 tablespoons cacao powder

Growing up as a kid, I was never really sure if I liked Bounty bars. I think it may have been a texture thing. But then, y'know – you grow. Tastebuds grow and change, and I found myself having one hell of an addiction to coconut rough chocolate (essentially just milk chocolate laced with coconut – dangerous stuff). It was either that, or the fact that there were always a copious amount of chocolate bars lying around the house due to school fundraisers. (That's if my mum hadn't eaten them all... this one's for you, mum!) Nonetheless, I wanted to recreate that devilishly good combination of chocolate and coconut and have it for breakfast. And so, a Bounty Smoothie was born.

1. Blend the smoothie ingredients in a high-speed blender until creamy.

2. Whisk the ganache ingredients in a small bowl until all the lumps are gone.

3. Pour half of the smoothie into a jar, followed by a layer of ganache.

4. Alternate between these layers until you fill your jar.

5. Decorate with extra desiccated coconut (optional).

CHOC-MINT SMOOTHIE

MAKES
≪···1–2···≫
SMOOTHIES

For the chocolate layer:
2 frozen bananas, broken
    into chunks
125ml (½ cup) plant-
    based milk
250ml (1 cup) coconut water
2 tablespoons cacao powder
1 tablespoon coconut sugar

For the mint layer:
2 frozen bananas, broken
    into chunks
250ml (1 cup) almond milk
125ml (½ cup) coconut water
2 tablespoons pure maple syrup
1 teaspoon vanilla powder
1 teaspoon green spirulina or
    matcha powder (for colour)
1 drop of high-quality food-
    grade peppermint oil

To decorate:
melted vegan chocolate
mint leaves

Chocolate mint is a fantastic flavour combination and it seemed silly to not turn it into a smoothie. The creamy chocolate smoothie layer, paired with the freshness of the mint is to die for.

1. Blend all of the chocolate layer ingredients together in a high-speed blender until smooth. Pour into a separate jar and set aside. Rinse the blender.

2. Blend the mint layer ingredients until smooth and creamy. Adjust the liquid ratios to achieve your desired consistency. (Less liquid will result in a creamy, ice cream-like texture.)

3. Chill a jar in the freezer for 5 minutes, then drizzle some melted vegan chocolate inside to decorate.

4. Pour alternate layers of the chocolate and mint smoothies until you have filled the jar. Top with mint leaves. Enjoy!

COCONUT COFFEE

1 young green coconut,
cracked open
1 shot of quality espresso
coffee

Simplicity at its finest. You'll need a good coconut and a good shot of coffee. Trust me, you'll want to try this one. I know this sounds like a crazy combination, but it's seriously amazing. If you love coconuts and love coffee, you'll love this.

1. Take a few sips out of the coconut.

2. Pour the shot of coffee into the coconut.

3. That's it. Drink and enjoy.

COOKIES & CREAM SMOOTHIE

MAKES
1
SMOOTHIE

For the 'cookie' pieces:
65g (½ cup) almonds
2 tablespoons cacao powder
20g (¼ cup) desiccated
   coconut
115g or 6 Medjool dates, pitted

For the creamy smoothie:
2 frozen bananas, broken
   into chunks
125ml (½ cup) coconut cream
250ml (1 cup) almond milk
2 teaspoons vanilla bean
   powder
2 tablespoons maple syrup
   or rice malt syrup

Cookies and cream ice cream was a staple of mine growing up. Honestly, it wouldn't be surprising to see me devouring nearly a whole family-sized tub in a sitting. Or, I'd be the person that would have gone through the whole tub of ice cream and simply eaten all of the chocolate cookie chunks. I have no regrets. And I know you won't regret this smoothie! Creamy, delicious and it's like ice cream.

PS – I highly recommend investing in some vanilla powder. It tastes incredible and it adds a subtle sweetness I guarantee you will love.

1. Firstly, you want to prepare your cookie pieces by pulsing the almonds, cacao powder and coconut in a high-speed blender or food processor until a fine meal forms. Add the dates last and pulse until it begins to stick together. Set aside in a bowl.

2. To make the smoothie, simply blend the bananas, coconut cream, almond milk, vanilla and maple syrup in a high-speed blender until creamy. Adjust the liquid as needed.

3. Break the cookie pieces into small chunks and add to the blender again. Pulse the smoothie a few times to break the pieces up a little more.

4. Pour into your favourite glass jar and serve at once.

GOLDEN 'MILKSHAKE'

SERVES
《···1–2···》

125ml (½ cup) chilled
    coconut cream
250ml (1 cup) water
125ml (½ cup) chilled
    almond milk
60g (½ cup) raw cashews,
    soaked for 3–6 hours
4–5 tablespoons coconut
    sugar (or sweetener
    of choice)
1 teaspoon ground cardamom
1 teaspoon ground cinnamon
1–2 teaspoons ground
    turmeric
1 teaspoon pure vanilla
    bean paste or powder
¼ teaspoon salt

Loaded with the amazing benefits of turmeric (think powerful antioxidant and anti-inflammatory properties) and paired with creamy cashews and the warmth of cinnamon and cardamom, you honestly can't go wrong. I love storing this milkshake in the refrigerator and just sipping away at it whenever a sweet craving appears. This milk also steams wonderfully, so feel free to warm it up via a steaming wand or over the stovetop to change things up a little!

1. Blend all the ingredients in a high-speed blender until smooth and all the lumps are gone.

2. Pour into a jar and serve. Store any leftovers in the refrigerator in a sealed bottle for up to 5 days.

OPTIONAL:

For a smoother 'milk', feel free to press this through muslin or cheesecloth with your hands. However, with a high-speed blender, you should be able to blend the cashews completely.

NEAPOLITAN SMOOTHIE

MAKES
1
SMOOTHIE

For the base:
2–3 frozen bananas,
    broken into chunks
1 tablespoon maple syrup
1 teaspoon pure vanilla
    extract with seeds
250ml (1 cup) almond milk
175ml (⅔ cup) water or
    coconut water, plus
    more if needed

For the strawberry layer:
100g (½ cup) frozen
    strawberries

For the chocolate layer:
1 tablespoon cacao powder

I will readily admit I was that annoying child who ate only the chocolate and strawberry flavours and left the vanilla for whoever was last to get to the tub (sorry, not sorry). Anyway, enjoy sipping through three mesmerising layers of deliciousness.

1. Make the base by blending the frozen bananas, maple syrup, pure vanilla extract, almond milk and water until smooth and creamy.

2. Pour around three-quarters of the mixture out into a separate bowl. With the remaining one-quarter of the mixture in the blender jug, add the frozen strawberries and blend until creamy. Add a little more water if it becomes too thick (i.e. not moving through your blades).

3. Pour the strawberry layer into a medium-sized glass jar, then rinse your blender.

4. Next, pour half of the mixture that you have reserved in the bowl gently on top of the strawberry layer (for the vanilla layer). I used a spoon to ensure I was able to get clean, separate layers.

5. Pour the remaining smoothie mixture back into the blender and blend with the cacao.

6. Gently spoon this on top of the vanilla layer. You should have three gorgeous, creamy layers!

PEANUT BUTTER & JELLY SMOOTHIE

MAKES
1
SMOOTHIE

For the raspberry layer:
50g (½ cup) frozen
    raspberries, partially
    thawed
1 tablespoon raspberry jam
60ml (¼ cup) maple syrup

For the peanut butter layer:
2–3 frozen bananas, broken
    into chunks
250ml (1 cup) almond
    or cashew milk
125ml (½ cup) coconut
    water or water, plus more
    if needed
1 teaspoon pure vanilla
    extract with seeds
2–3 tablespoons peanut
    butter, or more, if you're
    anything like me

Nothing goes past me when it comes to peanut butter and jelly. Relish this sweet explosion of heaven for breakfast, lunch or dessert.

1. Prepare the raspberry layer by blending the raspberries, jam and maple syrup in a high-speed blender until smooth. Add a little water if needed.

2. Rinse your blender jug and then blend your peanut butter layer ingredients until smooth and creamy.

3. Pour a small amount of the peanut butter layer into a jar, followed by a generous dollop of the raspberry layer. Alternate between these two layers until you fill the jar to the top (or run out of smoothie). Serve immediately topped with a dollop of peanut butter and a few raspberries.

PIÑA COLADA SMOOTHIE

MAKES
1
SMOOTHIE

For the creamy coconut layer:
2–3 frozen bananas, broken
  until chunks
20g (¼ cup) desiccated
  coconut
125ml (½ cup) coconut milk,
  plus more if you'd like
250ml (1 cup) coconut water
1 teaspoon pure vanilla
  extract with seeds
1 tablespoon coconut sugar

For the pineapple layer:
150–160g (about 1 cup) fresh
  pineapple chunks
1 frozen banana, broken
  into chunks
60ml (¼ cup) coconut water
1 tablespoon coconut sugar

To serve:
desiccated coconut
pineapple slices (optional)

'If you like piña coladas'… However, respectfully, I don't want to promote them at 8am for Sunday breakfast. (You can ,however, and I won't judge you.) I will offer this as a substitution, just don't get caught in the rain with it, will you?

••

1. Blend the creamy coconut layer ingredients in a high-speed blender until smooth and creamy. Set aside in a jar.

2. Rinse your blender jug and then blend the pineapple layer together until smooth and creamy.

3. Grab an empty jar, and begin pouring alternate coconut and pineapple layers into the jar until you have used all of both.

4. Dust your smoothie with a little desiccated coconut and serve with a wedge of pineapple (optional).

SNICKERS SMOOTHIE

MAKES
《··· 1–2 ···》
SMOOTHIES

For the caramel layer:
1 ripe banana
5–6 Medjool dates, pitted
60ml (¼ cup) almond milk
1 tablespoon peanut butter
1 tablespoon almond butter
½ teaspoon salt
1 teaspoon pure vanilla
   extract with seeds

For the vanilla nougat layer:
2 frozen bananas, broken
   into chunks
250ml (1 cup) almond
   or cashew milk
125ml (½ cup) water
½ teaspoon pure vanilla
   extract with seeds
   or powder

For the chocolate ganache:
80ml (⅓ cup) coconut
   oil, melted
30g (⅓ cup) cacao powder
60ml (¼ cup) maple syrup
pinch of salt

To decorate:
crushed peanuts

*Also pictured here is a Raw
Snickers Bar. You can find
the recipe on page 246.*

Layers of rich caramel, chocolate and creamy vanilla – this is
killer. Enjoy this jar of dreams for breakfast, as a sweet snack
or as dessert.

. . . .

1. Begin by preparing the caramel layer. Simply blend the
ingredients for the caramel in a high-speed blender or food
processor until creamy and smooth. Set aside in a bowl.

2. Prepare your chocolate ganache by whisking together
the coconut oil, cacao powder, maple syrup and salt until
all the lumps are gone. Set aside.

3. Rinse your blender jug and then blend the vanilla nougat
ingredients until thick and creamy.

4. To assemble your smoothie, begin by drizzling the chocolate
ganache around the jar. Begin to alternate between spooning
layers of caramel and the creamy vanilla nougat smoothie mixture
into the jar. Once you have used up all of your smoothie mixture,
top with a final layer of caramel, some chocolate ganache and
some crushed peanuts. Add some extra decadence with a
Raw Snickers Bar.

STRAWBERRY SHORTCAKE SMOOTHIE

MAKES
1
SMOOTHIE

For the strawberry layer:
100g (1 cup) fresh
   strawberries, plus extra
   to garnish
60ml (¼ cup) rice malt syrup
   or maple syrup

For the vanilla layer:
2–3 frozen bananas, broken
   into chunks
180ml (¾ cup) almond mik
125ml (½ cup) coconut cream
80ml (⅓ cup) water,
   plus more if needed
1 teaspoon vanilla bean
   powder

For the shortcake sprinkle:
2 tablespoons almonds
2 tablespoons pecans
2 tabelespoons desiccated
   coconut

Frozen strawberries are just next-level amazing, and paired with the creamy vanilla smoothie and the crunchy shortcake sprinkle – it's a match made in heaven. Go on and treat yourself for breakfast, or even dessert!

1. Blend the strawberry layer ingredients together in a high-speed blender and set aside.

2. Pulse the shortcake sprinkle ingredients in a food processor until a fine meal forms and also set this aside.

3. Rinse your blender jub and then blend the vanilla layer until thick and creamy. Add more liquid if you'd like to adjust the consistency.

4. Time to assemble! Simply fill a jar to the halfway point with the vanilla layer, then top with some of the strawberry layer then a sprinkle of the shortcake. Simply repeat this process until you reach the top of your smoothie jar, finishing with a shortcake layer. Garnish with fresh strawberries.

5. Enjoy immediately. Eat with a spoon and thick straw to enjoy the delicious crumble layers.

WATERMELON CRUSH

MAKES
《⋯ 1 ⋯》

800g–1kg fresh watermelon
(around ¼ of a large
watermelon)
200g (1 cup) frozen
strawberries
juice of 1 lemon
small handful of mint leaves

To decorate:
watermelon wedge
mint leaves
lime wedge

This is a jar of liquid summer-happiness-joy-love-everything.
It's SO delicious, so refreshing and it's one of my staples when
trying to cope with Melbourne heat. Watermelon is great for
your digestion and your skin, so blend this up and rehydrate!

1. Simply blend all the ingredients in a high-speed blender
until the mint leaves have fully blended.

2. Enjoy in a chilled glass jar, decorated with a wedge of
watermelon, a couple of mint leaves and a wedge of lime.

INDEX
•••

ACKNOWLEDGEMENTS

•••

Mum & Dad: Thank you for everything you sacrificed for me. Even though we live an ocean away, I will always be grateful to have been (and still be) loved so fearlessly.

Josh: I wouldn't be who I am without you. Thank you for being my rock not only whilst writing this book, but for life. Thank you for taking care of me, for listening to and loving me unconditionally and for being the best taste-tester I could have asked for. I love you.

Aliza & Caitie: Your unconditional love, friendship and generosity means the world to me. Thank you from the bottom of my heart for everything you have both helped me with, because without you this book wouldn't be nearly half as magical. And without you, I fear that my fridge would be overflowing with too much food.

Paul & Kate: I am eternally grateful for the trust, generosity and friendship you both give me! Thank you for giving me the creative space to make this book possible, for believing in me and for supporting my dreams in a way that no other people could.

Charlie & Peach: My babies – Mum misses you! (Yes people, these are my cats, and yes you bet that they are reading this book). Thank you for showing me what unconditional love is. Meow.

Evan, Shane, Andy, Saul, Angie, Belinda, Amber & the rest of the New Zealand crew: I love you guys. Thanks for always inspiring me to be a better person, for all the laughs, fun times and gratitude you have shown me since we first met. Our friendships have shaped me into who I am today.

Kim AKA @bestofvegan: For always being my #1 donut fan, and for your generosity in sharing my work with the world via social media. Without you I wouldn't have been gifted with the amazing opportunities that I have.

To Oli & the Blink Publishing team: Thank you for believing in me and allowing me to pour my heart and soul onto these pages.

Sam Murphy lives in Melbourne, Australia, by the beach. By day, she works as a vegan chef, and this passion tends to spill into her home life as well. Believing that food is truly there to be enjoyed, Sam spends much of her spare time in the kitchen creating recipes, feeding those around her and spreading her love of delicious food to the world.

Instagram: @sobeautifullyreal